Critical Acclaim for *Life Is a 4-Letter Word*

"David Levy has nailed what it means to glean all the greatness out of life's masterful lessons."

— **Kristine Carlson**, co-author of the Don't Sweat the Small Stuff books

"Professor David Levy's book is insightful, profound, funny, and thoroughly original. Meaning in life is everywhere, he reminds us, and whether it changes us profoundly or sails right over our heads, it's nice to know it's there."

— **Lewis Colick**, screenwriter (*October Sky*, *Ghosts of Mississippi*, etc.)

"David Levy's warm, funny and wise reflections on his life's journey offers both comfort and hard-won advice for readers looking to improve their own lives."

— **Dennis Palumbo**, therapist, screenwriter (*My Favorite Year*), and author (*Daniel Rinaldi Mysteries*)

"Levy has masterfully gleaned wisdom of the ages and packed them into bite-sized and thoroughly enjoyable morsels of literary delight."

— **Tom Greening**, Editor Emeritus of the *Journal of Humanistic Psychology*

"Dr. Levy's brilliant, touching, and humorous collection of stories showcases his well-honed, multi-faceted skills as a storyteller, educator, and psychologist. Readers will delight at the relatable snapshots of people, relationships, and events and find wonderful treasures of expertly distilled learning points embedded within."

— **Judy Ho**, board certified clinical and forensic neuropsychologist, associate professor, and author (*Stop Self-Sabotage*)

"Meticulously crafted, these engaging, funny, and often moving vignettes perfectly set up the brief but potent shots of distilled wisdom that follow."

— **Drew Erhardt**, psychologist, codeveloper of the *Moodnotes* and *MoodKit* apps

"A tour de force of wisdom nestled in a pithy, enjoyable and profound package."

— **Louis Cozolino**, author (*Why Therapy Works* and *Timeless*)

"This is a very special book that I predict will find thousands of eager readers. The stories combine David Levy's wonderful sense of humor with insights and wisdom about life. It is well written and a kick to read!"

— **David N. Elkins**, psychologist and author (*The Human Elements of Psychotherapy*)

"Life is short. You can either suffer the pitfalls of life's lessons on your own — or you can learn those lessons by reading Dr. Levy's sharp-witted and insightful book."

— **Marilee Bradford**, producing director, The Film Music Society

"Chicken soup, with a few dashes of Tabasco, and laced with scintillating humor."

— **Eric Shiraev**, cultural psychologist, George Mason University

Also by Dr. David A. Levy

Tools of Critical Thinking

Cross-Cultural Psychology

Family Therapy (Russian translation)

LIFE
>IS A<
4-LETTER
WORD

LIFE

>IS A<

4-LETTER

WORD

**Laughing and Learning
Through 40 Life Lessons**

DR. DAVID A. LEVY

CORAL GABLES

Published by Mango Publishing Group, a division of Mango Media Inc.

Cover & Layout Design: Elina Diaz

For permission requests, please contact the publisher at:

Mango Publishing Group
2850 S Douglas Road, 2nd Floor
Coral Gables, FL 33134 USA
info@mango.bz

For special orders, quantity sales, course adoptions and corporate sales, please email the publisher at sales@mango.bz. For trade and wholesale sales, please contact Ingram Publisher Services at customer.service@ingramcontent.com or +1.800.509.4887.

Life Is a 4-Letter Word: Laughing and Learning Through 40 Life Lessons

Library of Congress Cataloging-in-Publication number: 2019948609
ISBN: (print) 978-1-64250-154-4 , (ebook) 978-1-64250-155-1
BISAC category code SELF-HELP / Personal Growth / Happiness

Printed in the United States of America

To my mom and dad, who are in every one of these essays — even the ones they aren't.

To my kids — Jacob and Briana.

To Mary Jane — at long last, true love.

And to the memory of Zorro Levy.

TABLE OF CONTENTS

FOREWORD

LIFE — DON'T SWEAT IT

David Levy has nailed what it means to glean all the greatness out of life's masterful lessons in his new book, *Life Is a 4-Letter Word*. Laugh along with him, as I did, while drinking in these warm-hearted anecdotal stories that will help you keep life in perspective.

KRISTINE CARLSON, co-author of the
Don't Sweat the Small Stuff books

PROLOGUE

THE SHOT

I can still remember the antiseptic smell of the doctor's office and the feel of the cold metal examination table underneath my naked six-year-old legs. My white jockey shorts provided the only shroud of protection and dignity I had left, barely buffering me from utter humiliation. My mom sat close by, patient but helpless.

Of course, every kid hates shots. But I *especially* hated shots. The mere thought of that cold, shiny, spiky tool of torture nearly paralyzed me with terror. But I was also a very verbal kid. And when I was anxious, I'd talk. *A lot.* It was my best defense — in fact, frequently my only defense.

The nurse's name was Gabe. I know that because I can vividly picture that ominous name embroidered in dark red stitching on her crisp white uniform. Outside of the office, Gabe was probably a decent enough woman. But when armed with that wicked weapon, Nurse Gabe was nothing more to me than a heartless bureaucrat, whose only function was to inflict her merciless will on me before moving on to the next hapless child.

The door flung open with a thud, followed by Nurse Gabe, holding The Shot with the nonchalance of a mailman merely delivering the next package. Instantly, I felt that familiar raw panic coldly surging through my tiny veins. She made her approach, ready to stab me with her bayonet. I counter-attacked with a barrage of questions: "No, wait! What kind of shot is it? Wait! Is it a booster shot? Wait, wait! Is it a tetanus shot?" Nurse Gabe turned to me and said simply but firmly: "David, you can ask me all the questions you want. *But you're going to get the shot.*"

She had me. Checkmate. I realized there was nothing more I could do or say. I had run out of escape routes. I reluctantly offered her my arm, wrenched my head away, scrunched my eyes, held my breath, and prayed it would be over quickly… which, to my surprise, it actually was.

Don't get me wrong, it was really bad. But not nearly as bad as the gut-wrenching agony of all that *waiting*. When there's no getting around something, it's best just to go through it. And when it's inevitable, the sooner the better.

INTRODUCTION

Although my experience with The Shot happened nearly sixty years ago, it still lives inside me. And the lesson I took from it has carried me through decades of life's challenges: *Why put off the inevitable?* In a very profound sense, Nike had it right: "Just Do It."

The power of this lesson inspired me to start collecting other stories from my life that captured some important moral. Whenever I'd recall one, I'd grab whatever was handy — a Post-It note, a scrap of paper, a napkin — and scribble down a few key words as a reminder:

- *what do women want?*

- *beat by a computer at tic-tac-toe*

- *press button for better sound*

- *you are NOT going to Disneyland!*

- *the booby prize of life*

One by one, I would place them into a folder labeled *LIFE LESSONS*, stash it in my filing cabinet, and then get back to doing whatever it was I was doing.

Over the years, the folder became thicker and thicker, eventually brimming with dozens of notes. I hadn't given much thought to what I was going to do — if anything — with them. But I knew they were important to me.

On occasion, in my work as a psychologist and a professor, I'd share a few of these anecdotes when they seemed relevant. I was struck by how frequently they resonated with others. I came to realize the impact of these stories is a result of their being both *personal* and *real.*

Gradually, the collection of ideas metamorphized into the form of a book. I decided at the outset that I did not want this book comprised of my experiences as a therapist working with clients. There are several such books out there — many of them quite good. Instead, I envisioned a book that reflected experiences of everyday living, both ordinary and extraordinary: passing moments, distressing episodes, all kinds of occurrences that most people can relate to.

But how to organize these anecdotes? At first, I toyed with the idea of grouping them by themes: facing fears, letting go, envy, aging, life is grand, life sucks, and so on. However, as I amassed more and more of these stories, a different structure emerged. I saw that, when placed in roughly chronological order, they traced the arc of my growth, my development, my life — story by story.

As you pass through the gallery of these essays, I hope they will prompt you to reflect on your own stories and life lessons. Maybe you can even share them with others, as I've done with you…

P. S. The names used throughout this book are real. (Except those that aren't.)

THE CHALLENGE

"PLAY THE COMPUTER AT TIC-TAC-TOE." The innocent invitation was posted at a local corner shopping center one sunny Saturday afternoon. "Not much of a challenge," I smugly mused. "How hard could this be?" After all, I had long since mastered this game for tots.

Mind you, I wasn't exactly sure what a computer actually was. But no matter. This was the early 1960s, I was nearly eight years old, and everything was possible. It was going to be a battle of the ages: *Boy versus Computer*. And I was gonna kick the computer's electronic butt.

I confidently strode into the exhibit tent, which was sponsored by IBM or Bell Labs, or some other creator of futuristic technological wonders. As I took my place in line, my eyes were drawn to a massive sign hanging ominously above the computer screen: "YOU CAN'T BEAT IT. SEE IF YOU CAN TIE IT." I scoffed at the very notion, utterly convinced that I could figure out a way to slay this pompous behemoth.

I approached the massive, soulless black screen. The primitive white cursor blinked at me arrogantly, daring me to make my move. I was not to be intimidated. I took a deep breath, and The Challenge was on…

Game 1: Tie. ("Okay, you've got this covered.")

Game 2: Tie. ("Come on, you can do it!")

Game 3: Loss. ("What the…?")

Game 4: Loss. ("This *can't* be happening!")

Game 5: Tie. ("Okay, now don't panic.")

And so it went…seemingly random sequences of losses and ties. But not one win. As my veneer of denial began to slowly erode, the realization crept up my back like an army of cold spiders: *I could not win*. But, surprisingly, after the initial frustration, a tie started to feel not-so-bad; as a matter of fact, it felt pretty good. (Or at least, it felt acceptable.) There was no such thing as a "win." A tie was a win. I walked home alone that day, humbled but wiser. Tic-tac-toe was never the same again…

But this was more than just a game of tic-tac-toe. It turned out to be about all kinds of challenges. Especially challenges in important relationships, like with friends, family, or partners. It's not about "winning." In fact, when you "win," you usually don't really win. (You actually lose.) And when they "win," they don't really win. (They actually lose.) The best outcome is a tie. If you can both walk away equally satisfied — or even equally dissatisfied — that's the real challenge. And the real win.

LIFE LESSON:

SOMETIMES A TIE IS REALLY A WIN.

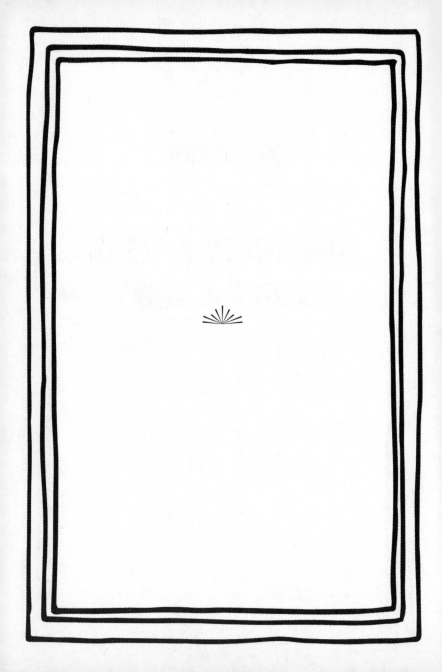

THE NATURE OF ATTACHMENT

Clearly, someone didn't think this one through. It's as inevitable as heartbreak in Hollywood. Puppies grow up to be dogs. Kittens grow up to be cats. And our family's pet ducklings — Huey, Dewey, and Louie — grew up to be ducks.

What did *we* know about nature? We were a middle-class Jewish family living in a middle-class neighborhood in Inglewood, California, in the early 1960s. And we had just acquired three adorable hatchlings which we kept in a box in our garage. What could *possibly* go wrong?

It all started so perfectly idyllic. My dad tenderly teaching us how to provide them with food, water, and shelter. My younger siblings and I chasing the pocket-sized birdlings around the lawn of our little backyard. Their awkward waddling on those little flat feet and those high-pitched quackettes. And when we held them in our tiny hands, carefully cradling the soft puffs of yellow down against our bare skin…well, it was almost too much bliss for a child to bear. I thought it would last forever.

But of course, it didn't. One day my dad took me aside. "David, our pets are growing up. We have given them a wonderful home, but they need to be with their friends and start families of their own. They will always love us, and we will always love them, but soon it will be time for them to return to their place in nature."

Well, the only thing even close to "nature" in our neighborhood was Alondra Park — which happened to have a large pond populated with a multitude of assorted ducks. One fateful day, with mixed emotions my dad and I packed up Huey, Dewey, and Louie in the back of our white Pontiac station wagon and shepherded them to their new home.

When we arrived, my dad and I gently guided them to the pond, then turned to head back to the car. But something was very wrong…We noticed our faithful pets waddling in tight formation right behind me. "*Daaad!*" I wailed. "They're following me!" And so it went. Back to the pond. Back to the car. Back to the pond. Back to the car. But each time, with increased urgency. I was beside myself. Finally, we made a break for it. My dad scurried me to the car, we flung ourselves into the seats, and sped off, tears pouring down my face, and my poor dad looking absolutely miserable.

Despite what "they say," these ducks did *not* take to water…nor anything else in this foreign land. And despite the best of my dad's intentions, his mission was doomed to fail long before it even began.

It wasn't until many years later when I was studying for a psychology class in college that I first read about "imprinting" in birds — how young hatchlings become instinctively attached to the first animal or object that they see near them, which they then identify as their parent. This is how they learn to navigate through life, by observing how the trusted parent behaves. Evidently, little Huey, Dewey, and Louie were simply doing what their DNA instructed them to do: They had imprinted on me — I had unknowingly become their parent. And that day in Alondra Park, when faced with the uncertainty of their new environment, they diligently shadowed me, imitating my every move, searching for direction from their trusted parent.

But imprinting can occur in other species too. In puppies. In kittens. And, in a way, in kids. Looking back on it, I had imprinted on my dad. By observing how he behaved, I absorbed the values of caring for the helpless and vulnerable. Of respecting nature. Of saying good-bye to things you love because it's best for them...even if it hurts. And most important, trying to do the right thing when life goes awry...in fact, *especially* when life goes awry.

LIFE LESSON:

DOING THE RIGHT THING CAN BE PAINFUL.

THE EMPTY THREAT

It was a stressful morning at "The Happiest Place on Earth." The lines were long, and the tempers were short. Although it was still morning, the heat was already sweltering, and the air was thick with the bedlam of manic kids and the already-frayed nerves of beleaguered parents. And this was just waiting to buy a ticket.

My family — parents, siblings, and I — had woken up early that day to make the expedition from Los Angeles to Anaheim in our station wagon. Brimming with excitement, we trekked our way through the never-ending parking lot toward the grand entrance. We ever-so-slowly snaked our way toward the turnstile. The anticipation was excruciating. Then, just beyond the bars of the front gate, we finally caught our first magnificent glimpse: Lo and behold, The Magic Kingdom!

But thwarting our passage into the Promised Land was The Chaos Family: three unruly youngsters and two haggard parents. The oldest kid — he looked to be about seven, maybe a couple of years younger than I — was being particularly rambunctious. His arms, legs, hands, and mouth all seemed to be traveling in different directions simultaneously. (And this was *years* before ADD had become all the diagnostic rage.)

The mother was clearly on her last nerve. In sheer desperation, she snapped, "If you don't behave, we are *not* going to Disneyland!" The kid froze in his tracks and locked eyes with his mother… for all of about one second. During that momentary sliver of time, it was truly remarkable how much that kid conveyed without ever uttering a single word: "Yeah right, Mom." "Oh, *this* again." "How stupid do you think I am?" "That's pathetic." "Did somebody say something?" He then promptly returned to his business of being an out-of-control, unruly kid — as if the exchange never even happened.

Once I became a parent myself, I grew to have much more empathy for that poor mother. I now know what it's like to feel utterly desperate, frenzied, and powerless. But I also understand — even somehow admire — her kid's reaction. In his eyes, she had long since lost all credibility. And with it, his respect. Empty threats are worse than none at all. And that brief but powerful look he shot her…I never want to be looked at like that. Sadly, however, it really doesn't matter what I want. Being a parent, you somehow just find a way to get used to it.

LIFE LESSON:

EMPTY THREATS ARE WORSE THAN NONE AT ALL.

BRIDGING THE RACIAL DIVIDE

White versus Black. Black versus White. It was the late 1960s, and Morningside High School was undergoing the growing pains of racial integration. Although the fires of the 1965 Watts riots — located just a few miles to our east — had been doused years before, our school was still smoldering with racial tension. Stresses and strains permeated the campus. Walking through hallways could be hazardous. Restrooms were rife with hidden dangers. Heated interracial fistfights would spontaneously erupt in the quad lunch area, with spectators feverishly rooting for their favored combatant — based solely on skin color.

But for one week that fall, things felt…different. We were about to face off in our annual football game against our cross-town rival to the north: Inglewood High. This promised to be more than your typical "rah-rah" game of high school football, however. You see, Inglewood High didn't have a single black student. And that fact held profound meaning that was not lost on any of us at Morningside.

That week, as if by magic, interracial boundaries at our school were dissolving, ousted by a newfound sense of shared purpose and meaning. Black and white students were now smiling and chatting with each other. Rancorous disputes were replaced with enthusiastic conversations. The sounds of Sly and the Family Stone's "Everyday People" reverberated through the halls and permeated our souls.

The night of the Big Game, the atmosphere at the stadium was teeming with the aroma of hotdogs, popcorn, and hope. We were galvanized and we were mighty. Colors had been realigned: No longer was there segregation of black and white — only unity under the red and white banner of our beloved Morningside Monarchs. The racial divide had been bridged by a collective purpose against a common foe. The stakes couldn't have felt higher — for we were rooting not just for our team on the field, but also for racial harmony within our school and across the land.

From the opening kickoff, we fought hard. We fought tough. We fought close. And we lost. *We lost.*

Honestly, the game was played fair and square — we simply got beat by the better team. The final score was right; but the final outcome was so *wrong*. Deeply wrong. Symbolically wrong. Morally wrong. If this were a just world, we would have emerged victorious. But for us, there was to be no justice…only bitter defeat.

Shell-shocked and disillusioned, we numbly filed out of the stadium, our collective hearts shattered into a million splinters.

And adding to the misery of that wretched night, we were forced to endure the spectacle of our opponents' jubilant celebrations spilling out from their stands and onto the field. Had this been a movie, it would have been an absolutely rotten ending.

Of course, it was tempting to demonize the students at Inglewood High as somehow being the enemy of racial tolerance. But that simply wasn't the case. I actually had a number of friends who went there, and I knew that they were good, decent people (I mean, as much as your typical teenager could possibly be). No, the kids at Inglewood were just high school students — like us — who happened to be on the winning side of a lousy football game.

Over the next week, a sense of emptiness and despair was palpable across Morningside High. Sure, we'd all heard the adage that "life isn't fair" over the span of our relatively short lifetimes. From almost our first moments of consciousness, everybody is exposed to a never-ending barrage of unfairness — whether at home, school, or play. But this was an exceptionally gut-wrenching reminder. For this was not just your sister getting a bigger slice of cake, or you not getting selected for the school play; no, this was a direct assault on the very concept of moral justice.

Nevertheless, having the camaraderie of others who were experiencing the same feeling was a salve that somehow helped to soothe our pain. And slowly, time began to heal the wounds.

I can't say that it mended all racial divides. But there was noticeably less tension and fewer conflicts around the school. We were scarred and deflated, but now bonded — through the agony of a shared defeat. Hard times can forge stronger ties than cheerful times.

Oh, and by the way, a few weeks later, Morningside squared off against another non-integrated high school — this one from an affluent area on a hill several miles to our south. During this contest, many students in their crowd were less than civil. They taunted us with verbal insults and Confederate flags. I don't actually recall the score; but I do remember that we pummeled the snot out of them. That conquest — at least for that one night — felt like unfairness had been vindicated. (And it would have made a *much* better ending for a movie…)

First, together in defeat; now, together in victory. Life is not fair, but it's easier in unity. *"Power to the people, right on!"*

LIFE LESSON:

LIFE ISN'T FAIR — BUT IT'S EASIER WITH COMPANIONSHIP.

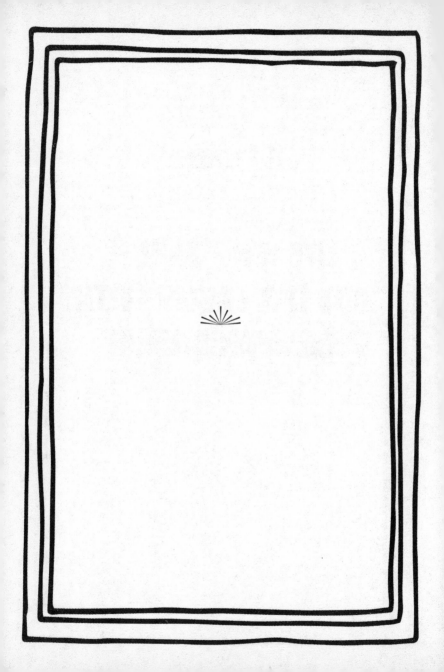

"...AND NOTHING BUT THE TRUTH"

The courtroom was cold, ominous, and intimidating. But naturally I couldn't show how I felt. I was sixteen years old and was not about to appear as anything other than aloof and bored. My poor mom was both nervous and embarrassed as we approached the judge's bench...

Having been issued a traffic ticket the month before, I was making my mandated court appearance. Evidently, the engineers at Fiat had neither the foresight nor courtesy to design their mid-1960s two-seat convertible to accommodate a driver and five teenage passengers. After rehearsals for our high school production of "The Skin of Our Teeth," I'd hastily lower the top and cram as many cast members into the car as possible — some of them wedged behind the seats and some onto the trunk — and ferry them home. The nightly rides were sheer joy. But one evening, the buzzkill of those flashing red lights abruptly swung our collective mood from unbridled ecstasy to deep gloom. And although I was definitely bummed out, I really can't say that I was surprised.

The judge pondered something for a couple minutes, then admonished me for my behavior, let me off with a warning, and dismissed the case. My mom breathed an audible sigh of relief, thanked him, and we headed toward the exit. But, *dammit*, I just couldn't leave well enough alone. Much to my mother's chagrin, I turned back, overcome by an uncontrollable need to stand up to The Man and get in the last word: "Excuse me, Your Honor," my voice dripping with sarcasm, "but I didn't realize that there was any particular law against the number of people I can carry in my car."

The judge's look was stern, but his voice was kindly: "But you knew it was *wrong*, didn't you, son?" He had me. I had nothing to say. No flimsy excuse. No convoluted rationalization. No smartass teenage retort. Nothing. My juvenile swagger had dissolved into humbled silence. I simply lowered my eyes and nodded slowly.

Of course, he was right. He knew it. My mom knew it. Everybody in the courtroom knew it. And, most important, I knew it.

It's easy to rationalize irrational behavior — it gives us comfort. It's much harder to seek and accept the truth — it can be painful. And recognizing the difference between the two can be harder still. But if we value truth over self-deception, it's well worth the pursuit.

LIFE LESSON:

DEFEAT RATIONALIZATIONS WITH TRUTH.

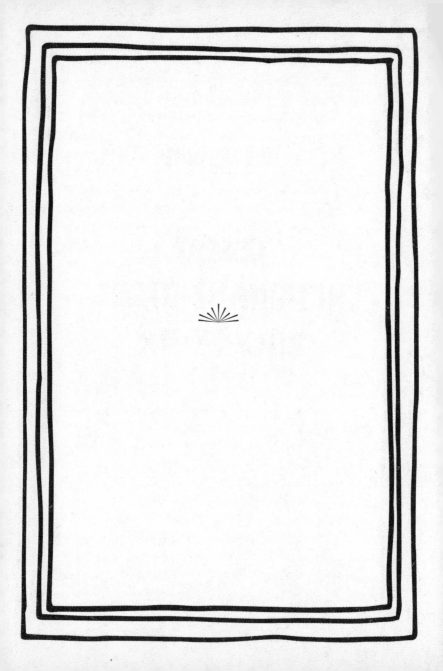

WORSE AND WORSER

The price was right. Ever since it first opened its doors, the LA Free Clinic was a welcome refuge for those lacking in either medical insurance or financial resources — which, as a recent college graduate in the mid-1970s, was me. Once there, you could seek assistance for everything from a dog bite or sprained ankle to hepatitis or pregnancy testing. All you had to do was walk in, provide the quasi-hippie chick behind the counter with your name, reason for visit, astrological sign (no, I am *not* making that up), and then wait…and wait…and wait…

As I settled into a hard plastic chair on that faded linoleum floor, I noticed against the wall, a large wooden rack, chock full of educational pamphlets, all arranged in alphabetical order. Since I had nothing but time and anxiety on my hands, I perused each one, working my way from A to Z. Allergies. Breast Cancer. Coronary Heart Disease. Diabetes. Epilepsy.

When I reached Venereal Diseases, I thought, "Okay, let's see what's happening in *that* world." The first page covered gonorrhea; the second, syphilis. The brochure was loaded with basic medical information, accompanied by some disgustingly graphic illustrations. Then I got to a sentence that, even to this day, still sends shivers down my spine: "Of course, one can contract both gonorrhea *and* syphilis in the same sexual encounter." (Boy, talk about your rotten luck!) My mind raced to one possible scenario:

FADE IN:

INTERIOR: COUPLES' BEDROOM — NIGHT

HE

Baby, I have some really bad news…

SHE

What is it, sweetie?

HE

…and I hope that you'll be able to forgive me.

SHE

It's okay, you can tell me. I'll always love you. No matter what.

HE

Well…I just found out that I tested positive for gonorrhea. And I probably gave it to you.

SHE

What?! How *could* you?!

(choking back tears)

You miserable piece of shit!

(now sobbing uncontrollably)

HE

You're right. I am a miserable piece of shit. But I hope you can find it in your heart to forgive me.

SHE

Forgive you? How could I *ever* forgive you?!

HE

I'm not sure. But I pray that you can. You mean everything to me. I'll do *anything* to make things up to you.

SHE

I don't know. I just don't know.

(sobbing again)

You're such an asswipe! I *trusted* you!

HE

Please? I beg you, *please*?

SHE

(after a pause)

All I can say is that I'll think about it.

(wiping away her tears)

I mean, I don't want to throw away our whole relationship.

HE

Thank you, thank you, *thank you* baby. I love you *so* much!

SHE

I love you too. We'll find a way to work this out.

HE

I know we will.

(after a pause)

Oh, baby…?

SHE

Yes, sweetie?

HE

Umm…there's just *one more little thing…*

FADE TO BLACK

As anyone who knows me would testify, I am by nature anything but an optimist. For some, the glass is half full. For others, the glass is half empty. I used to joke that for me, there is no glass.

However, over time and with mindful effort, I have found that it is possible to gradually shift that perspective in a more constructive direction by focusing on worse case circumstances. Fever of 101? Well, it could be 104. Can only afford to buy one new pair of shoes? It could be zero pairs of shoes. Having a squabble with your partner? At least you *have* a partner. When someone says to me, "Well, at least it couldn't be any worse," my rejoinder is usually swift and firm: "*Don't say that!* Things can *always* get worse!" (And, frankly, at some point in the future, they very likely will be.)

I don't recall what actually brought me in to the LA Free Clinic that day. But I do remember what I came away with: The knowledge that, no matter how bad things are, they could always be worse — so, try to be grateful that they aren't. And the price for that nugget of wisdom was, fittingly, free.

LIFE LESSON:

THINGS COULD ALWAYS BE WORSE.

THE ZEN STRIPPER

"Exotic Dancers." What an odd euphemism. Had someone misspelled the word, inadvertently swapping an "r" with an "x"? Didn't matter. The pink-and-turquoise neon sign hypnotically flashing outside the red velvet curtain beckoned me. I was barely twenty-one when I anxiously stepped foot into this surreal environment. I clumsily made my way to a red leatherette booth that was as far from the stage as I could possibly find. The music was thumping and there were scantily clad girls chatting and laughing and milling about everywhere. It was absolutely terrifying — and terribly exciting. I gazed forward, praying to be seen and yet not seen. Trying to appear as cool and calm as a secret agent in a foreign land. Within moments, I felt a warm body sit beside me. I could barely summon the courage to see who it was.

She was an older woman. You know, like twenty-six or something. And very pretty. Okay, now what was I supposed to do? "So…what's your name?" I awkwardly asked, not having any clue where to look or not look. "Vixen," she replied with a wink and a smile. "Oh. Umm…is that your real name?" I stupidly inquired. (James Bond I clearly was not.) "Of course not, silly! It's Karen."

I was instantly intrigued. And no, not only for the obvious reasons. I found everything about her fascinating. "What was it like, the first time you went on stage?" She tilted her head. "Well, that was years ago. But I remember feeling nervous and embarrassed. I really wanted everyone's approval, but I was afraid of being rejected — Ya know, not being good enough. And lots of shame and guilt…I kept thinking about what if my family could see me." "And then what?" I quickly queried. (Remember, when I'm anxious, I ask lots of questions.) "Well," she began, "the moment I heard all of that cheering and clapping, and saw the dollar bills raining down on me, I felt great!" "And what about since then?" I wanted to know. "Well, I've been doing this for a long time. I guess by now I'm pretty much used to it. It's my job. Yeah, it can get weird — what I do for a living, the long hours I spend in this place, all the alcohol and drugs in the dressing room, the parade of faceless strangers, staring at me from the darkness. This is my life."

I was now completely immersed in her story. I needed to know how she copes with all of it: "What about now? How do you survive?" She shrugged, paused a moment, and replied simply: "Three minutes at a time." And, as if on cue, her song began. Karen gave me a pat on the leg, and Vixen made her way to the stage.

So that was how she did it. I got it. It's just too overwhelming, trying to take on everything all at once. Break it into smaller chunks and try to live more in the present. "Three minutes at a time." Kinda like the X-rated version of Alcoholics Anonymous. (But with happier customers and better tips.)

LIVING IN THE MOMENT MAKES LIFE MANAGEABLE.

TESTING THE LIMITS

It was utterly surrealistic. In a heartbeat, the once-proud Alfa Romeo roadster had been reduced to a smoldering heap of mangled metal. *Did this really just happen?* One moment, gliding and slithering around bends. *How could this be?* The next moment, slamming into a concrete embankment, spinning out, and wheezing its last breath. *When was I going to wake up from this nightmare?*

Ever since I saw the movie *The Graduate*, the image of Dustin Hoffman rocketing up and down the California coast in pursuit of his True Love in his 1967 Alfa Romeo convertible became my quest. All I needed was the means…

And then along came *Wonderbug*. In 1976, I had landed a television series: essentially *The Mod Squad* for kids — with the added bonus of a magical dune buggy named Wonderbug. So, it was only fitting that a magic car enabled me to get my own magic car.

And it was truly a thing of beauty. Fully restored…from its sleek, red body to its immaculate aluminum engine. I bathed, and polished, and waxed it past the point of obsession. Every imperfection — even a squashed gnat on the windshield — was immediately remedied.

I hadn't had my Alfa for more than a few precious months. Early on Sunday mornings, I'd test her limits on the empty roads in the hills outside of Los Angeles. She drove like a dream: smooth, nimble, and spry.

One curve in particular begged to be challenged. I mean, it simply needed to be conquered. And Alfa and I were not to be denied. I wondered, how fast could my baby take this curve? Determined to find out, I began to experiment, gradually increasing the speed with each trial. Pushing and pushing the limits. *How fast could I take this curve?* One fateful morning, I found out. I hit the limit. And the wall.

I had once fantasized about zooming up the Pacific Coast Highway in pursuit of my True Love. Instead, I ended up demolishing my True Love on a barren hill. With no one to blame, but myself.

How close can you clip your fingernails? Is the paint dry enough for you to touch? How deep can you dig before you hit the sprinkler line? Do you give the screw just *one* more twist? Should you toast the bagel just *little* bit longer? Should you give your lips just *one* more collagen injection? Is it safe to have just *one* more drink? Should you give your partner just a *little* more "honest feedback" about their appearance? Should you try just a *little* bit harder to seduce your date?

In short, *how do you know when you've gone too far?* The answer, unfortunately, is when you've gone too far.

Sure, it's challenging — and sometimes even fun — to push the limits. But at what cost? Are you willing to pay the price of your risk/reward miscalculation? You can always toast another slice of burned bread or mend a broken sprinkler line. Not the same for totaling your car. Or violating someone else's trust. Or jeopardizing your life. We test the limits at our own peril.

One pretty reliable way to err on the side of caution is not to put yourself in a position where you're even tempted to push the limits. In my case, my very next car was also a convertible — but this time, not a little Italian sports car. Instead, it was a 1965 Chevy Impala — with all the size, girth, and nimbleness of a WWII Sherman tank. And, *voilà*! Temptation: nonexistent.

LIFE LESSON:

YOU ONLY KNOW YOU'VE GONE TOO FAR WHEN YOU'VE GONE TOO FAR.

A SHORT STORY

Growing up short — to borrow Bette Davis's line about growing old — isn't for sissies. But it's especially rough when you're a guy. The ache of watching everybody else in gym class predictably being chosen before you. The dread of approaching the height-requirement bar at amusement parks. The sting of watching your friends joyously riding roller coasters as you force a pained smile across your reddened face. Perhaps worst of all, the humiliation at your first school dances, slow dancing with a girl who'd tower over you like a Women's NBA All Star awkwardly embracing a nervous jockey.

Genetics being what they are, countless generations before me were also vertically challenged. My dad was, of course, no exception. In my early twenties, still plagued by this struggle, I asked him for some words of wisdom. He confessed that it used to bother him so much that, one day when he was around my age and courting my mother-to-be, he slipped into a store specializing in "Elevator Shoes for Men." My eyes widened in amazement. Maybe there was some hope for me! I implored him to tell me every detail.

He recounted that as he sat down to get fitted, he noticed an older gentleman — sporting a stylish suit and tie — in the chair next to his. Even though they were both seated, the guy still looked a foot taller than my dad. He was, in fact, so tall that my poor dad had to crane his neck up just to make eye contact. The man's height was everything my dad desperately wanted to have. "Excuse me sir, how tall are you?" my dad inquired. The man smiled and replied, "I'm six-two." My dad was baffled: "Then why are you getting these elevator shoes?" The man responded with a shrug, "I want to be six-four."

I had asked my dad for some words of wisdom. And he provided them to me. But not about being short. Instead, they were about the insatiable itch of envy…which can only be truly scratched by painstaking acceptance. Acceptance of oneself and even one's struggles. I got it. When it is "never enough," it's *never* going to be enough. (But I'd still like to be six foot two — hell, even five foot ten — for just a day…)

LIFE LESSON:

TRY TO REPLACE ENVY WITH SELF-ACCEPTANCE.

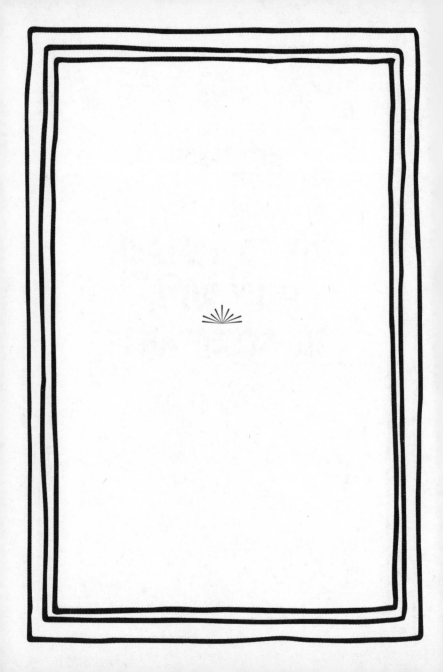

THE TICKING CLOCK

Once upon a time…before there was streaming video, there were DVDs; before DVDs, there was VHS; and before VHS, you actually had to go to the theater to see a movie that was "out of circulation" — in other words, virtually every movie that had ever been made. As an avid movie buff, I'd scour the *LA Times* every week, hoping to spot one or more of my all-time favorite classics. I was especially drawn to musicals: *The Wizard of Oz*, *West Side Story*, *Singing in the Rain*, *The Music Man*. I was also captivated by the animated Disney classics, like *Sleeping Beauty*, *Pinocchio*, *Fantasia*, and even *Peter Pan*. I loved them all.

So, in my early twenties, when I spotted the rerelease of *Cinderella* playing in limited engagement at local movie house, I eagerly seized the cinematic opportunity.

There I sat in the cocoon-like refuge of the theater, my buttered popcorn and Diet Coke in hand, swept away and mesmerized from the first notes of the overture. Everything was just as I remembered it as a kid. The beautiful and innocent Cinderella. The cruel and spiteful stepmother, stepsisters, and Lucifer the cat. The ever-loyal and sympathetic mice and Bruno the dog. The promise that she would be allowed to attend the Royal Ball, if only she completed all of her chores.

My heart broke for Cinderella as she wept softly in the garden, having just been tricked, humiliated, and then utterly betrayed by the evil stepmother — robbed of her only hope for happiness. (Hope can be a dangerous thing!) There would be no Ball for her. "There is nothing left to believe in. *Nothing*," she sobbed.

But then, in Cinderella's darkest moment, her Fairy Godmother makes her miraculous appearance. "Nothing, my dear? If you'd lost *all* your faith, I couldn't be here. And here I am!" (I yearned, *Oh, if only life worked this way!*) And, with a few swift strokes of her magic wand, she transforms a pumpkin into a carriage, the mice into horses, her horse into a coachman, her dog into a doorman, and her shredded dress into that magnificent blue gown.

Cinderella, overcome with gratitude, exclaims, "Why, it's like a dream — a wonderful dream come true!" Her Fairy Godmother's words are kind, but sobering: "Yes, my child. But like all dreams, well, I'm afraid this can't last forever. You'll have only 'til midnight. On the stroke of twelve, the spell will be broken, and everything will be as it was before."

And here is where the story unexpectedly took on a whole new meaning to me. As I sat alone and transfixed in the darkness of that theater, I suddenly felt as if I had been struck by one of those spectacular bolts of lightning from a Disney movie. In that instant, I knew that Cinderella now has a choice: She can begrudgingly show up to the Ball and squander the evening by obsessively fretting about its inevitable demise. Or, she can appreciatively attend the ball — knowing full well that it's *not* going to last — and try to immerse herself in the splendor of the experience, despite the inescapable ticking clock.

Instead of "dreams," her Fairy Godmother might as well have been talking about life itself. That it's *not* going to last forever. It *can't* last forever. And we all have only until "midnight" — no matter what we want, or wish, or desire. But we also face the same choice as did Cinderella. Do we lament and mourn the inevitable conclusion, long before it's even made its appearance? Or do we embrace being at the ball, for as long as it lasts? For us, the ball is *real*. And if we can accept that "real" doesn't mean *permanent*, we have a chance to live "happily ever after…" (At least, up until midnight.)

※

P. S. It wasn't too long thereafter that *Peter Pan* made a reappearance at my local theater…and, along with it, a somewhat darker version of a similar life lesson. The fearsome Captain Hook, as you might recall, sported a hook where his hand used to be. As the story goes, Peter Pan had cut off his hand and fed it to a hungry crocodile, who then developed a taste for the Captain's flesh.

So the only thing in the world that would send Captain Hook into an absolute PTSD panic was the prospect of a future encounter with the ravenous reptile, who pursued him relentlessly. And how did he sense when the dreaded crocodile was approaching? Well, it seems that the croc had previously swallowed an alarm clock…a ticking alarm clock. And Hook knew that when "time" caught up with him, it was going to tear him to shreds. *Tick…tick…tick.* Living in perpetual fear. Not exactly "happily ever after…"

LIFE LESSON:

YOU RISK LOSING THE PRESENT BY FRETTING ABOUT THE FUTURE.

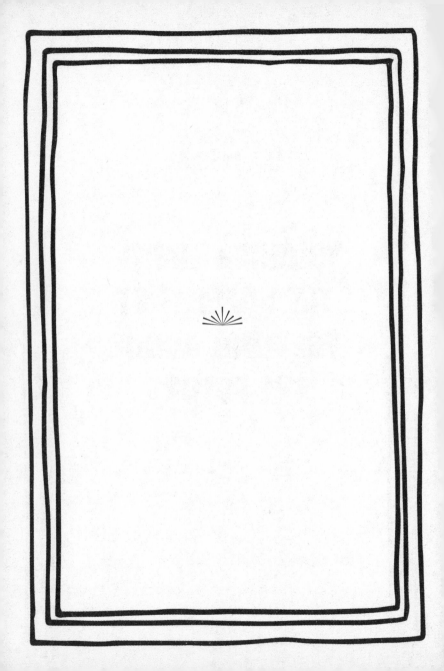

THE STONED WALL

The dude was a stoner. I mean, a *serious* stoner. We're talking first-thing-in-the-morning, last-thing-at-night stoner. An all day, every day stoner.

It didn't start out that way; it never does. In high school, he loved to "party" — but only when there were actual parties. By the time he graduated college, he no longer needed the pretense of a party. He just got stoned — wherever and whenever. In fact, I don't think he ever allowed himself to be un-stoned.

Everybody around him — his wife, his family, his friends — became increasingly troubled as they witnessed his steady descent into apathetic lethargy. But everyone was nervous about confronting him — no one wanted to create any turmoil. So, I took it upon myself to step up and have a real heart-to-heart talk with him. I let him know, first and foremost, that I cared about him. And that I was worried about him. His declining job performance. His physical health from smoking and his safety while driving. His agitated and depressive mood swings. The effects on those close to him. The disappointment of his wife. The role modeling for his kids. I laid it all out as clearly and convincingly as possible.

When I finished, there was a long pause. His eyes glazed over. (But then again, they were *always* glazed over.) He took a breath and attempted to muster some degree of earnestness: "Yeah bro, I hear ya. I *definitely* have to maybe start thinking about maybe cutting down or maybe something like that at some point…"

Well, that was the end of that. Words reveal intentions. I might as well have been talking to a wall…a stoned one.

He wasn't ready. In fact, he might *never* be ready. And the rude awakening was that nobody could really do anything about it. I had run smack-dab into the limits of control. Mine. And everybody else's.

If he wanted to change, it was up to him. It could all start with a decision, a commitment to take action. With that, we could help. Without it, we were helpless. We had to let go of our attempt to control the outcome. Even more disturbing was the realization that most things — and people — are beyond our ability to control. To assume otherwise is foolhardy and delusional. And we can put *that* in our pipe and smoke it.

LIFE LESSON:

RECOGNIZE THE LIMITS OF YOUR OWN CONTROL.

THE MARVELS OF CYNICISM

Life was good. My best friend Gino and I were basking in the glory of a beautiful Southern California July afternoon. We had recently graduated from college and were engaged in our customary summertime ritual: plopping ourselves on my orange and brown couch (this was, after all, the 1970s) in my tiny apartment, blissfully cruising through one TV channel after the next, and beginning to quarry our second pint of Haagen-Dazs coffee ice cream.

I was mid-spoonful when a commercial appeared on the air for a ballot proposition for the upcoming fall election. It was a beautiful thirty-second spot — crystal mountain streams, sapphire blue skies, dramatic golden sunsets — all laced together with a soothing musical underscore. The commercial didn't actually have anything specific to say — other than how I was supposed to cast my vote. My buddy's mood suddenly turned to one of outrage, vehemently proclaiming, *"Screw that! I'm not voting for it!"* I was taken aback. "But Gino, how can you make that decision? We don't even know what it's for, and the election is months away!" Without missing a beat, he retorted, "Anybody who can afford a TV commercial like that in July can't *possibly* have my best interests at heart!"

Turns out, Gino was right. Months later, the truth was revealed: The advertisement was for a ballot initiative sponsored and funded by some malevolent chemical company.

But, how did he know? Well, to start, Gino was the most well-read person I'd ever met, frequently plowing through two or three books at any given time. I had also always stood in awe of his lightning-quick mind. And he was a salesman by trade, often boasting "I can sell ice to an Eskimo!" Since he understood the subtleties of persuasion, his Bullshit-O-Meter is always on high alert.

But whatever the causes — and despite his generally upbeat nature — Gino's cynicism served him well. He was instinctively watchful for spotting hidden motives, embodied in the Latin phrase *cui bono*: "for whose benefit?" And in this instance, he smelled it miles away.

I had always prided myself on my skepticism — attempting to suspend judgment until I have more facts before drawing a conclusion. But sometimes, cynicism is the right tool for the job, penetrating like an X-ray to the hidden marrow of truth. And in countless situations, it pays to be ever-vigilant for the profit motive.

Of course, too much cynicism is a liability…it can lead to bitterness and despair. But when infused with just the right amount of humor, it can be a potent antidote to naiveté and gullibility. And serve as protective armor against those with less-than-honorable intentions.

A HEALTHY DOSE OF CYNICISM IS A POTENT ANTIDOTE AGAINST GULLIBILITY.

KISS QUEST

"It's simple, but not easy." I forget where I first heard that adage, but I've always liked it. Life is hard enough; no need to make it more complicated.

This notion was vividly driven home to me in my mid-twenties, when I was directing my first professional stage show, a musical review of the work of George and Ira Gershwin. All of us involved in the production — creators, cast, and crew — were about the same age. Both blessed and cursed with the unbridled self-confidence that comes only with youth, we didn't have the common sense to be scared out of our wits.

Our orchestrator, Francis, and our conductor, Matthew, each possessed remarkable musical talents. But they couldn't have been more different in temperament or style. Francis was cosmopolitan, philosophical, and suave (at least as much as a twenty-four-year-old could be). In contrast, Matthew was earthy, pragmatic, and socially rather awkward.

In creating a show, the orchestrator's job is to conceptualize how the music is to be arranged and how it should sound. The conductor's job is to interpret that vision into a musical performance. So Francis would do his best to express to Matthew exactly what he envisioned. And Matthew would do his dutiful best to comply.

But it was like witnessing two guys from different countries attempting to negotiate a contract, each in his own native language. Francis's words were abstract, metaphorical, and poetic: "I'd like this passage to be more wistful"; "I'd like that passage to be more effervescent." But Matthew, who tended to be more concrete and practical, couldn't quite follow. His eyes would glaze over, he'd tentatively nod his head, and then consistently fail to give Francis what he wanted.

And so it would go, week after frustrating week. It became increasingly clear that Francis was speaking a language that Matthew was entirely unable to translate. As Francis's patience waned, he tried making his appeals more nuanced — and more complex: "Please make it less ponderous and more ethereal." "This should be a blend of contemplative yet also yearning." Their communication divide only widened.

As opening night bore down on us, tensions were reaching a boiling point. Finally, Matthew summoned the courage to approach Francis — timidly but clearly: "Maybe we can just try sticking with the four basics? Do you want it *faster, slower, louder,* or *softer*?" At first, Francis was taken aback. He thought he had been crystal clear. But then he got it. At long last, understanding had been achieved. And with the first musical downbeat on the first night of the performance, both Francis and Matthew ultimately got what they each wanted. And so did the enthusiastic audience. But it wasn't easy getting there…

The value of pursuing simplicity has stayed me with ever since. I'm constantly reminded of it when I see people close to me struggle with all types of addictions. "It's simple, but not easy": Just don't pick up the bottle; it's not going to pour itself down your throat. Just don't grab the needle; it's not going to jump off the counter and stick itself in your arm. Just don't place the bet; the money is not going to flutter out your pockets and onto the gaming table.

None of this is meant to minimize the horrible pain and anguish of those who do battle with tortuous addictions. That's hard enough. But don't over complicate it. Strive for simplicity.

Years later, I discovered that this concept is embodied in what is known as the *KISS principle*: "Keep It Simple, Stupid." Although this amusing acronym was first coined in the early 1960s by a prominent aeronautical engineer as guidance for his aerospace designers, the KISS quest is universal. Or at least it should be…

LIFE LESSON:

SIMPLE IS BETTER — BUT NOT ALWAYS EASIER.

PASSING THE ULTIMATE BUCK

I know she meant to be kind. In fact, she didn't have a cruel bone in her body. We were in our mid-twenties, my girlfriend and I. She was talented, cheerful, and sincere…and also happened to be a born-again Southern fundamentalist Christian. Being Jewish, this caused me — and us — a not insignificant amount of dissonance. One warm summer evening, I took the opportunity, in a quiet moment walking along the shore, to ask her about her beliefs. I smiled apprehensively but warmly, "Julia, you don't really think I'm going to burn in hell, do you?"

"Sweetheart," she began, sadly shaking her head. Her eyes were full of a blend of compassion, pity, and wistful resignation. "It's not up to *me*."

Not the answer I was expecting. Or hoping for. My heart sank. And not because I was afraid she was right that I was going to burn in hell. (After all, if that's where I was headed, at least I wouldn't be alone…I'd be roasting with all of my friends and virtually all of my heroes.) No, what pained me was that I felt a grim disconnection: I couldn't make her "see" and she couldn't "save" me. We still cared about each other. But I realized that gap could never — *ever* — be bridged. It was a bittersweet sunset…

SOME GAPS CAN NEVER BE BRIDGED.

THE IMPOSTOR
SYNDROME

"David? Alfred. *What the hell am I gonna do?!*" The voice on the other end of the phone was immediately recognizable — infused with the flamboyance of James Brown and the sassiness of Little Richard. Alfred was the lead dancer in a musical production I was directing. And he was in a state of sheer panic. Our show was opening the next night, and poor Alfred was having a meltdown of epic proportions. "Let's be honest here," he implored, his voice quivering. "We all know I'm really not a dancer. And when I'm out there on that stage tomorrow night, *everybody* is going to find that out. I'm gonna be exposed as a *fraud*. An *impostor*. And in front of the LA Times — *The Times!*"

Mind you, Alfred possessed all of the attributes of a dancer. He had the body build of a dancer — long, gazelle-like legs and graceful arms. He had the attitude of a dancer — confident and charismatic. He even had the smile of a dancer — brilliant and dazzling, even from thirty rows back.

In fact, there was only thing he *didn't* have as a dancer: He couldn't dance. I'm not saying he was clumsy or awkward; far from it. He could learn basic dance steps, and, to his credit, he looked pretty fabulous doing them. Nevertheless, his confession was accurate — he really was not a dancer. No training. No skill set. Not even much experience.

I tried to calm him down, without betraying my own insecurity. (After all, his performance could reflect poorly on me as well… maybe he wouldn't be the only one to be exposed as an impostor.) I thought back to his auditions for the show. How could we possibly come to have cast him as a lead dancer? The fact is, he was able to sparkle, shine, and somehow pull the whole thing off. "Alfred," I began slowly, "I have to confess. You fooled me. And you fooled the choreographer, and the musical director, and the rest of the production team. You fooled all of us. So, you know what? All you have to do now is go out there tomorrow night and fool everyone else."

Alfred offered a half-hearted thank you, but I could tell I did little to quell his rattled nerves. As I laid in bed that night, tossing and turning, I flashed back to a game of dodge ball when I was five years old. It was the Kindergarteners versus the First Graders…and I was totally out of my league. Every one of my determined throws was successfully — and gleefully — dodged by all of the upper-classmen. They were having a blast; I was absolutely miserable. How could I ever hope to compete with six-year-olds, even in a not-so-friendly game of dodge ball?

My friend, Bernie Nap, who was in the first grade, took me aside. Sensing my discouragement, he put his arm around me and offered some elderly words of solace. "David, it's okay. Us first graders are good dodgers" — as if to say, "Don't feel bad about yourself. You're young. We're old. You don't stand a chance in hell."

Once I reached first grade, of course, it was an entirely different story. I had achieved dodgeball top dog status on the playground. (I even took some pity on the poor kindergarteners, who tried in vain to compete with "us first graders.") My sense of confidence was short-lived, however, lasting only until I was forced to play against the *second* graders. Then I reverted back to a state of frustration and futility. And so the cycle continued…

That plague of feeling totally out of my league — and feeling like an impostor — has revisited itself throughout my life, much like a disease that goes into temporary remission and then intermittently crops us, seemingly immune to a permanent cure.

We've all experienced similar feelings, whether it's the first week of classes, starting a new job, dating, parenting, or invariably, the opening night of a show…always living with the gnawing fear that one day, someone will finally spot us for who we *really* are: "I don't know how you made it this far. Looks like you were able to fool everybody else. But the jig is up. You don't fool me!"

I have yet to find a foolproof antidote for this malady. But I did discover that adopting an attitude of "fake it 'til you make it" was as useful as anything else.

And what happened with Alfred? After our opening night performance, many of us stayed out celebrating all night, awaiting the imminent reviews. I stumbled back to my apartment around six thirty in the morning and spotted a single blinking red light on my primitive telephone answering machine. Who could it be, at this ungodly hour? (Theater people never — and I mean *never* — wake up at the crack of dawn.) I pressed play, and there was the unmistakable voice: "David? Alfred. *I fooled the Times!*" (Click.)

And indeed he did. I tore open the morning paper to read a glowing review of our show — and a specific reference to Alfred as an obviously "*accomplished dancer.*" It spelled triumph and vindication. He faked it, and he made it. Not a bad formula for coping with the impostor syndrome.

WHEN YOU DON'T KNOW WHAT TO DO, FAKE IT 'TIL YOU MAKE IT.

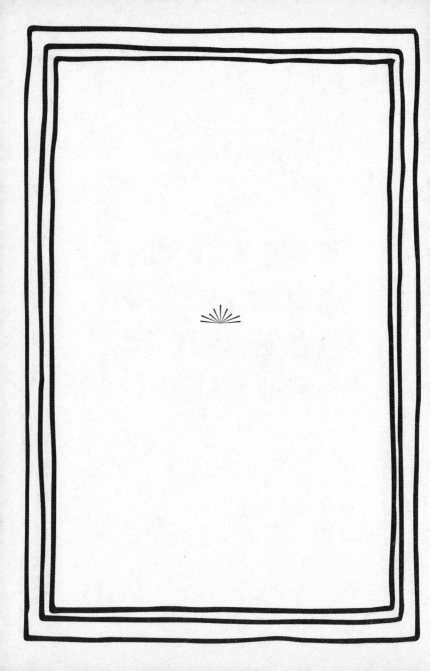

15-ZIP

The early eighties were awash with popular trends: *Pac-Man*, MTV, the mullet haircut, yuppies...and racquetball. I first discovered this game when my friend Jonathan (or "JP," as he was known), invited me to join him on a local court. I took to the game immediately. It's a fast-paced sport that's great exercise, relatively easy to learn, and, in the vernacular of the day, "super-fun" to play.

JP was an avid racquetball enthusiast. He played frequently and he knew the intricacies of the game, inside and out. Although I was a total novice, JP offered to provide me with weekly tutorials. He was a wise and patient teacher. He'd meticulously explain the various strategies and then relentlessly drill me on the assorted methods of attack: The passing shot. The ceiling shot. The pinch shot. The Z-shot. The kill shot.

Late at night, I'd head to the local racquetball courts and practice these shots for hours. Whenever I had the opportunity, I'd set up matches to play against my friends. And, sure enough, over the course of the summer, I got to be pretty good. But I could never even come close to competing against JP. This became more than a little discouraging.

"JP," I'd moan, "no matter how much I practice, I feel like I just can't make a dent in my game against you." His response was understanding and kind: "Big Dave," (yes, that's what my closest friends call me), "ya gotta keep it in perspective. It's all a matter of scale. I've been playing racquetball for years. And, honestly, I'm a really good player. So, sure, I can beat you 15-zip. But remember: There are guys out there who can beat *me* 15-zip. And there are guys who can beat *those guys* 15-zip."

The very idea was almost beyond my comprehension. How could *anybody* be *that* good? It got me thinking about other sports. I'd imagine the very best high school basketball player in the country. Then I'd imagine him going up against the very best college player in the country. Then that guy going up against the very best professional basketball player in the country. I was starting to get a handle on this whole idea of scale.

How about wealth? Okay, to me, a million dollars is *a lot* of money. But there are people out there who have ten million. And other people who have a hundred million. And still other people who have a billion. These individuals aren't simply "richer"… they are *orders-of-magnitude* richer. Suddenly, a million seems almost paltry by comparison…but certainly not to someone with "only" a few thousand.

Turns out, this principle applies everywhere. Jewelry. Cars. Engineering. Dance. Musicianship. It's all a matter of scale.

And what of the people who truly are at the top of the top? Those who can beat virtually *everyone* "15-zip"? Well, truth be told, I both admire and envy them. But I have to assume that in other areas of their lives, they don't beat others "15-zip." (Even Michael Jordan couldn't cut it in professional baseball.) In fact, I'll bet that in some instances other people actually beat *them* "15-zip." (At least it makes me feel a tad better to think so…)

IT'S ALL A MATTER OF SCALE.

HEDONIC GREED

It was 4:20 in the morning, the room was hazy, and JP and I shook our heads, laughing incredulously. I had recently purchased a new set of portable speakers for my Sony Walkman cassette player and was anxious to try them out. But of course, being the OCD guy that I was (and essentially still am), first and foremost I was compelled to meticulously pore over the full set of instructions. And there it was in the diagram, word-for-word: *Press button to improve quality of sound.*

Seriously?! What kind of "choice" is that? When would you ever *not* choose to press this button? JP and I tried to concoct some scenario when you might seductively nuzzle up to your sweetheart on a moonlit night and gently croon, "Baby, I'm kind of in the mood for some crappy sounding music tonight...What d'ya say?"

People love the idea of choice and control, we mused. Especially when it requires very little effort. And particularly when it seems like there are no costs. But this little damn button wasn't a *real* choice — it was a pseudo-choice. Hell, when would you not want *anything* to be "better"? JP and I were now on a roll:

When would you *not* want a better night's sleep?

When would you *not* want better tasting food?

When would you *not* want more pleasurable sex?

When would a man *not* want to feel more virile or a woman more attractive?

When would you *not* want to feel stronger, healthier, or more energetic?

We couldn't think of a single exception to wanting to feel better…even if "just little bit" better." JP and I mulled this idea over for a while. Maybe it explained the alcoholic's one-size-fits-all rationalization for drinking:

"It's been a great day — I want to celebrate with a drink."

"It's been a horrible day — I've earned the right to a drink."

"It's been a boring day — I might as well have a drink."

It all seems to be about seeking pleasure. In a word: hedonism. We wondered aloud if hedonism is inescapably hard-wired in our nature. Then again, to quote a line from the movie *The African Queen*, maybe "nature is what we were put on earth to rise above." But, on the other hand…

Okay, enough! JP and I had hit the limit of our 4:20 ponderings. Time to shut up and *finally* listen to some music. First up: "Don't Worry, Be Happy." (And, of course, we pressed the button to improve the quality of the sound. Some "choices" aren't *really* choices after all.)

BEWARE THE ILLUSION OF CHOICE.

THE SHELL GAME

I certainly have more than my share of character flaws, but gullibility isn't one of them. I have always prided myself on not being naïve. Gambling holds absolutely no allure for me. I am virtually immune to advertising. Salespeople might as well not waste their breath blathering about "the last one in the store," "for today only," "I have one of these myself," or, worst of all, "trust me." My motto has been *caveat venditor* — "let the seller beware."

That's why it was especially crushing when I fell — hook, line, sinker, rod, reel, and boat — for the oldest scam around: the classic shell game.

It was late afternoon on a pleasant fall day in Amsterdam. I had been meandering my way around Europe — traveling alone, crashing at sometimes seedy youth hostels — on a painfully constrained budget. For weeks, every dollar, franc, lira, and guilder was judiciously rationed out of my ever-shrinking fanny pack.

Suddenly my eyes and ears were drawn to a group of people, all whooping and hollering, huddled around a tiny makeshift table. As I made my way to the front, I immediately recognized the attraction.

One of the oldest cons in recorded history, the shell game is a sleight-of-hand trick, in which a pea is hidden underneath one of three walnut shells, cups, or, in this case, matchbox covers. The scam artist then quickly shifts the pea from one shell to another with the intent of deceiving the spectator into guessing — and incorrectly betting on — its location.

The action was frenzied. The youngish fellow seated behind the table sported a backward baseball cap, scruffy sneakers, and a pleasant Dutch accent. I was spellbound. His hands were quick, but not too quick; I was able to track his every move (or so I thought). I must have watched on for close to twenty minutes, as various spectators would win, lose, or walk away. And with every game, I was able to correctly guess (silently, of course) under which matchbox cover the pea had been placed.

My visceral excitement and self-confidence both were swelling. But did I have the gumption to actually wager some of my dwindling funds? I diligently scrutinized several more games — and each time, spotted the correct location of the innocent pea.

Okay, that did it — I just had to take my shot. (I mean, there was *no way* I could lose, right?) Since I had very little money in my pocket, I headed off to an ATM and impatiently withdrew twenty dollars. Not a fortune, to be sure. But, confident of my inevitable winnings, I would now be well-fed for the foreseeable future.

With hands trembling and heart pounding, I made my way back to the table. Finally it was time. The guy shuffled the matchbox covers a few times, then lifted the one on my left to reveal the pea. And then — and *I'm telling you the absolute truth* — in one clean, casual move he merely switched the positions of the left box with the middle box. And then asked if anyone wanted to wager.

I swallowed hard, uttered a brief Hail Mary (mind you, I'm Jewish), plunked down my twenty bucks, and pointed to the matchbox containing the pea. Without a trace of emotion, he lifted the cover and paused. My blood ran cold. *There was nothing there.* I stared in utter disbelief at the emptiness under the box — and the emptiness just stared right back at me. Surely my eyes were deceiving me. I blinked repeatedly — to no avail. "But it was just there!" I screamed silently. And now, it wasn't. The guy deftly scooped up my money and moved on, trolling for the next gullible sucker.

I had been swindled. Duped. Scammed. I slithered away, in utter humiliation — and with no one there to turn for solace. In a daze, I ambled back to my cramped hostel room, a stale granola bar, and my tattered copy of "Man's Search for Meaning."

So, lesson learned, right? Well, not *entirely*. Flash forward five years. The streets of New York City. A blustery winter afternoon. My chum, Drew, and I were wandering around, searching for a slice of the city's best pizza, when we turned a busy corner and chanced upon it: The Big Apple edition of the shell game.

The insignia on the backward baseball cap, sneakers, and accent all were different — but the game was unmistakably the same. The guy in Amsterdam was good; but this guy was *really* good. What especially captured our attention, though, was the group of spectators. As we watched on intently, we were able to detect that several of the onlookers crowded around the tiny table were, in fact, merely actors in the elaborately choreographed charade — both those who "won," and those who "lost." The whole intricate ruse was a marvel to behold.

Oddly, even with all of that knowledge, the game still somehow tempted us. "Since we know how it works, maybe we could outfox them?" we wondered aloud. But we swiftly came to our senses, realizing that these guys had surely planned for every possible contingency. *There is simply no way you're leaving that table with their money.* Lesson (finally) learned.

We all live with the fact that many "games" in life are rigged, in one way or another. Did you ever find out (usually too late) about the vast array of exclusions embedded in your insurance policies? Or try to challenge the multiple charges that are systematically stacked onto your monthly utility bills? And good luck navigating all the rights to privacy that you unwittingly sign away on the internet (have you honestly ever checked the box "Don't Agree"?) Frequently, there's little realistic option other than to participate. (Face it, you're not going to start up your own insurance, utility, or internet company.) In such cases, we need to live by the credo *caveat emptor* — "Let the buyer beware."

But, for God's sake, don't go out of your way looking to get ripped off. When you come across any situation that seems "too good to be true," as the saying goes, it probably is. Despite how tempting things might appear, you're not walking away a winner. The best action is no action: just don't play. And *caveat credulus* — "Let the gullible beware."

LIFE LESSON:

IF IT SEEMS TOO GOOD TO BE TRUE, IT PROBABLY IS.

EMPATHIC FAILURE

I entered therapy with such high hopes. I had recently made the life-altering decision to abandon my marginally satisfying career in show business to chart a new course in the field of psychology.

It wasn't an easy time. Despite being over thirty years old, I was back to being a student. I was still living alone in a cramped, single apartment. I had very little money. I was in a shaky romantic relationship. Nevertheless, I was brimming with newfound excitement about the prospect of a better and more fulfilling future.

In the course of my studies in graduate school, I became especially enamored with the theory of psychoanalysis. The voyage of deep self-reflection and examination was so appealing to me that I decided then and there that I needed to experience it first-hand. Sure, I knew that it would take a lot of work. And a long period of time. But I was fully committed to the challenge.

So, when I found an analyst who was willing to work for a significantly reduced fee, I was elated. Although he conducted therapy sessions out of his beautiful home office in the sweeping estates of Beverly Hills, Dr. Hermann's distinct Bronx dialect (not exactly Bugs Bunny, but in that general vicinity) revealed his roots in New York. Because of our common ethnic and religious ancestry, I felt we shared a deep understanding.

We spent over three years — like clockwork, every Monday afternoon — exploring the inner recesses of my dreams, my early childhood, my emotional complexes, and all things unconscious. The insights were fascinating, and the journey was exhilarating. I looked forward to every session.

But all that changed when reality reared its ugly head. By the beginning of my fourth year of therapy, my life began to unravel. I was quickly running out of money, my career was uncertain, and my relationship with my girlfriend was coming to an agonizing end.

I was sinking into the abyss of a deep and relentless depression. And once it had me in its crushing grip, it refused to let go. Food tasted like cardboard. Sleep was fleeting. Waking up was unbearable. My first thought every morning was about going to bed that night. I staggered through the day like a zombie wandering through a thick gray fog. It felt like a slow death by suffocation of the spirit.

I racked my mind for some way out. But no matter what I did, I couldn't find relief or comfort anywhere…just perpetual darkness, the minutes crawling like hours, and the hours crawling like days.

It was fortuitous that I was already in therapy and grateful that I had a place where I could go to seek respite from my anguish. I shared all of this with my analyst. His responses were predictably psychoanalytic: He wanted me to talk about my mother. And my father. And my childhood. And my unconscious. And, of course, my dreams. I reluctantly complied, hoping against hope that this might provide me with some relief. But it was like trying to find my way out of a dark forest wearing lead boots and equipped with a penlight, a broken compass, and a map of the wrong territory.

Week after futile week, my frustration grew. Dr. Hermann may have been giving it his psychoanalytic best — but it simply wasn't working. Finally, perhaps in desperation, he shifted from his traditional approach, by counseling me directly: "David, just do something that makes you feel better." This was as insulting as it was obvious. (As if I hadn't thought of that!) But I still tried to give him the benefit of the doubt. He had known me intimately for nearly half a decade, seemingly hearing every detail of my existence. So, I plaintively asked him what he recommended. The guidance he offered still reverberates in my psyche: "David, I'll tell you what I do when I'm depressed. I work in my garden. Or I take my son to the ball game. Or I make love to my wife."

My head snapped back in utter disbelief. With pulse pounding and stomach churning, I played his words back in my brain just to make sure I heard them correctly. *Had he not been listening to what I'd been saying for the past four years? Did he not know what my life was like…or even who I was??*

Before I even had time to formulate a response, the words came tumbling out of my mouth: "Okay, I'll tell you what Dr. Hermann. The next time I'm depressed, I'll be happy to come over to your house and work in your garden. And take your son to a ball game. And make love to your wife." (Except I didn't say "make love.")

With the passage of time and some positive life experiences, my depression eventually remitted. But Dr. Hermann's profound empathic failure that day marked the beginning of the end of my relationship with psychoanalytic therapy — and my analyst.

Oddly, it wasn't until over a quarter of a century later, when I sat down to write this story, that I actually started feeling kind of sorry for the guy. Sure, his words were shockingly insensitive and deeply invalidating. But if they lacked empathy, I have to assume that his intentions weren't unkind. In retrospect, he was in way over his head, and he didn't possess the knowledge, ability, or self-awareness to help me. To judge him too harshly would be like faulting a talentless actor for a lousy performance.

In other words, Dr. Hermann wasn't the only one who struggled with empathy. I'm not saying he is without blame. He had clearly failed me — on multiple levels — and he should have known it. At the same time, with this new understanding and perspective came the realization of my own shortcoming in empathy all these years…for him. (But I still maintain that it was an *astonishingly* dumbass thing for him to say.)

FIND FORGIVENESS THROUGH EMPATHY.

TINCTURE OF TIME

"Ouch, this really *hurts*!" I limped my way into Urgent Care, my ankle swollen and sore from a particularly ferocious game of racquetball the previous evening. I had prayed that it would feel better by morning. "Prayers do get answered," I reassured myself. And when I awoke, I found that my prayers had been answered. Unfortunately, the answer was a resounding "*No!*"

The doctor's eyes were kind. His voice, comforting. His demeanor, calm and gentle. It was as if Morgan Freeman had been transported from the movie screen to the examination room.

He carefully inspected my tender ankle. "Racquetball, huh? Fun game," he mused. As he perused the Twilight Zone-esque images of my X-rays, he concluded, "Well, looks like it's just some irritation or a minor sprain from your racquetball addiction. Nothing serious."

"Okay that's fine, but what do I do about it" I pleaded. His response was slow and steady: "We'll wrap it, you should ice it and elevate it at home, and just give it some time."

"Time?" I howled in my own head. "Who has time for *that?!*" Didn't he understand that I needed this damn thing fixed, and *pronto*? Hell, I had some serious racquetball to play! So, of course,

I peppered him with questions: "Can it be shrunk? Should I see a chiropractor? Is there some type of quick outpatient surgery?"

He smiled at me, with almost a wink. "The two best healers in this room right now are Mother Nature and Father Time."

I semi-nodded, "I think I know what you're talking about. But, seriously, *what are you talking about?*"

"Patience," he calmly replied. "There's not a whole lot you can do to make this better. But there are lots of things you can do that could make it worse. So, just don't do them."

As he carefully wrapped up the wounded ankle with a support bandage, I suddenly flashed back to my youth: playing outside with my friends / falling and scraping my knee / fighting back tears / making a bee-line for home / seeking the assistance and comfort of Mom / her drying my tears, cleaning the wound, covering it with a Band-Aid, cautioning me not to pick at it, and gently ordering me to go back outside and play. It was remarkable how — in that brief encounter — my mother was able to provide me with a permanent template for empathy, problem-solving, guidance, and a mandate to live life. *Dammit!* Mom was *right!* And sitting in the exam room with the doctor all those years later, it all felt so strangely familiar.

As I hobbled out to my car, my ankle was still throbbing. But somehow the pain eased with the wisdom of Morgan

Freeman, MD — and that of Mom. For wounds in life — physical or emotional — get some care if you need it. However, if you just have the good sense to stay out of the way, they will usually heal on their own. And for God's sake, don't make things worse; for if you keep picking at a scab, it will surely bleed. And maybe most important, don't stop living while you're waiting for things to heal.

It was time for me to "get back out and play with my friends." (And now, racquetball would just have to wait patiently for my return…)

LIFE LESSON:

THE TWO BEST HEALERS ARE MOTHER NATURE AND FATHER TIME.

IT'S JUST A FOUR-LETTER WORD

"What do women want?" This question has baffled men for millennia. Although I am not a fan of Freudian theory, I have to confess that I felt a certain degree of kinship with *Herr Doktor* when I learned that this mystery plagued him as well, evidently throughout most of his professional — and personal — life.

In my first year of graduate school in psychology, this topic was the fodder for passionate, and sometimes fierce, classroom debates. The consensus was that although men have their own idiosyncrasies, they are, by comparison, relatively simple creatures. But there was no resolution as to what drives women.

I became thoroughly obsessed. For weeks, I was a man on a mission. I asked every woman I knew — and even women I'd never met before — "What do you think women want?" I heard it all: "To be understood." "To be taken care of." "To be adored." "To be respected." "To be rescued." "To receive equal pay." "To be listened to." "To be worshipped." "To be ravished." "To be loved."

Then very late one night, I was at a friend's apartment, listening to some music with his roommate, an eccentric thirtysomething woman named "Birdie." Although this was the early 1980s,

Birdie looked like a remnant from the Woodstock era — replete with fringe jacket, tie-dyed tank top, and free spirit. Hoping that Birdie would have something unique to say about all of this, I posed the question to her. She took a slow swig of her Southern Comfort. Then, with a knowing smile and a twinkle in her eye, she replied, "Oh, I know what they want." My curiosity was piqued: "Okay, what? Ya gotta tell me!" She responded with cool confidence: "It's just a four-letter word."

This was big. Was one of the great mysteries of the universe about to be revealed to me? Was I going to peer into the inner recesses of the feminine psyche? The anticipation was excruciating. My mind raced…What four-letter word could it be? Was it "love?" Was it the linguistically crasser version of "sex?"

Her response froze me in my tracks: "M-o-r-e." I didn't understand. "More *what*?" I implored. She shrugged, grinning from ear to ear. "Whatever. More whatever." "But," I countered, "what if they're asking for *less* of something?" She replied, "Then do more of *that*." By now, my brain was sloshing around like a Maytag washer in overdrive: "You mean, 'more' includes doing 'more less'?" She looked gleeful, almost triumphant, as she readjusted her macramé headband, and sauntered off to the kitchen to pour herself another two fingers of whiskey.

When I saw Birdie a few days later, I mentioned that her insight really had a powerful impact on me. She looked puzzled and asked me what I was talking about. So, I recounted every detail of our conversation. Her eyes widened. "Did I say that? Hmm. Oh, well." As if it never even happened…

Was she just drunk? Was she toying with me? Did she really reveal a profound truth? Was it all of the above?

Well, I'm not saying that Birdie was right. And I'm not saying that she was wrong. But I do know that "what do women want?" seems as elusive as ever — destined to take its place in the pantheon of other age-old questions, akin to "what is the nature of creativity?" "what is the meaning of life?" and "what is the origin of the cosmos?" And while we busy ourselves pondering these imponderables, I think it wise not to get a bloody head from futilely bashing it against a wall. Some things seem destined to remain unknowable.

THE ANSWERS TO SOME QUESTIONS ARE DESTINED TO REMAIN UNKNOWABLE.

UNCOOL EFFORT

The lady doth protest too much, methinks.

— William Shakespeare, *Hamlet*

In the summertime, Venice Beach in Los Angeles is a veritable freak show — and I mean that in a good way. Vendors and vagabonds, healers and stoners, skaters and surfers, fortune tellers and body builders, tourists and street performers, all randomly milling about on the Boardwalk. Everyone is so different that almost nothing seems unusual…except one fellow who happened to catch my eye on one sizzling Sunday morning.

He looked to be in his mid-twenties, slightly overweight, and somehow just didn't seem to "fit in" — even in this eclectic mix. He was sporting a pair of very dark shades, about a dozen heavy gold chains around his neck, an entirely black urban wardrobe — including his oversized leather jacket and floppy beret — and not one but *two* Rottweilers, both dragging him down the Boardwalk on a leash, nearly pulling his arm out of the socket.

And he was trying to act like he didn't care. About anything. His dogs. How he looked. What people thought of him. Trying so hard…*too* hard.

What was he trying to cover up? Maybe his biggest fear was not standing out. Or of being average. Or of looking weak and vulnerable. But whatever it was, he was doing an awful lot of work to make it look like none of it mattered to him — which it clearly did. It was like he was communicating both "I don't give a shit if you look at me" while at the same time "For God's sake, *please* notice me." You just don't do that much work if it doesn't matter. It makes me suspicious when people "try too hard":

Vehemently insisting how easy-going they are.

Angrily declaring not to be angry.

Loudly boasting of being non-judgmental.

Fiercely objecting to being called narcissistic.

Aggressively swearing that they can be trusted.

Excessively broadcasting proclamations of love.

Wearing over-the-top clothing, makeup, and jewelry.

Or fervently denying unacceptable thoughts or desires — in other words, to "...*protest too much.*"

It's all so much work. To cover what? To compensate for what? I'm not always sure. But it's definitely *something...*

LIFE LESSON:

TRY HARD — BUT NOT TOO HARD.

THE BOOBY PRIZE

Her lips and tongue were still black from remnants of the activated charcoal they forced down her throat in the emergency room to neutralize the effects of the bottle of aspirin she had gobbled. Her wrists were tightly wrapped with surgical gauze and tape to stem the bleeding and sanitize the wounds from her self-inflicted cuts. And there she lay in the ICU, barely recovering from her thwarted attempt to take her own life.

How was this even *possible*? Gretchen was in her mid-twenties, bright, attractive, and seemingly had the world at her feet.

We were working together as interns at a local counseling center. We both were relatively new to the field of psychology and shared the excitement of altering our respective career paths — mine in entertainment, hers in sales. Gretchen was an intensely passionate woman, brimming with dedication and enthusiasm. So, needless to say, it came as a complete shock to me when I found out that she had attempted suicide late the previous night.

I dashed to the hospital the moment I heard the news, and anxiously found my way to her room. And there she was. It was definitely Gretchen…or at least a sunken and hollow version of Gretchen.

I quietly sat at her bedside, gently placing my hand on her shoulder. She looked up, recognized me, and was able to barely squeeze out a smile.

What the hell am I supposed to say in a moment like this? "I'm glad that you're okay"? (Yes.) "I'm so sorry that you're in such emotional pain"? (Yes.) "I'm confused and angry that you did this to yourself"? (Well, I certainly thought it — but I wouldn't actually *say* it.)

I didn't know Gretchen all that well, but I hoped she'd appreciate me not beating around the bush. "Gretchen, if it's not too personal…can I ask you why you were feeling so bad that you would do this to yourself?"

Her voice was weak, but the words were clear. "Well…I've sure given it a ton of thought. I know that I've always felt this deep void that goes way back to my early childhood. My parents clothed me and fed me, but I never felt seen by them. Or emotionally connected to them. So, I unconsciously developed a dysfunctional attachment style. It makes being intimate with others terrifying…but I still really crave it. I think it comes down to a core fear of abandonment." I was dumbfounded by her keen awareness.

She continued, "Over the years, I learned to develop a social façade to compensate for how lonely and empty I feel on the inside. And when I get close to people now, I have a lack of object permanence — so long as they're in my physical presence I feel safe, but the moment they're gone, it's like they're *gone*… as if they don't even exist. And when that happens, I'm gripped with panic. It's learned helplessness — that no matter what I do or try, it won't make any difference."

And she wasn't done. "I also didn't have good role models for healthy relationships. So I never learned how to have one. Then there's the genetic part…depression runs throughout my mom's side of the family. There's probably more, but that's my understanding as of now."

I nodded, speechless. Man, was I impressed! Her knowledge went way beyond anything I was learning in graduate school.

I let her know that I was pulling for her and offered my assurance that I would help in any way I could. I gave her a gentle squeeze on the shoulder and headed out the door, still in awe at her deep self-understanding. When suddenly, I was clobbered over the head with an entirely different thought: *What damn good was all of that insight? She just tried to kill herself!*

I came to realize that our ability to understand something does not necessarily enable us to change it. Moreover, insight into the "root" of a problem does not invariably solve the problem.

Gretchen's insight didn't buffer her against crushing pain and the impulse to end her life. But my insight — into the limitations of insight — turned out to be valuable.

I'm not saying that insight isn't important. It can be a useful, even indispensable, tool to help solve problems and alleviate human suffering. But it clearly has its limits.

What is a better solution? I don't know for sure. For some, it's taking action. For others, it's pursuing happiness or searching for meaning. Or maybe it's something else entirely. But insight alone? Sorry…despite its many virtues, insight may just be the psychological booby prize of life.

LIFE LESSON:

INSIGHT HAS FRUSTRATING LIMITS.

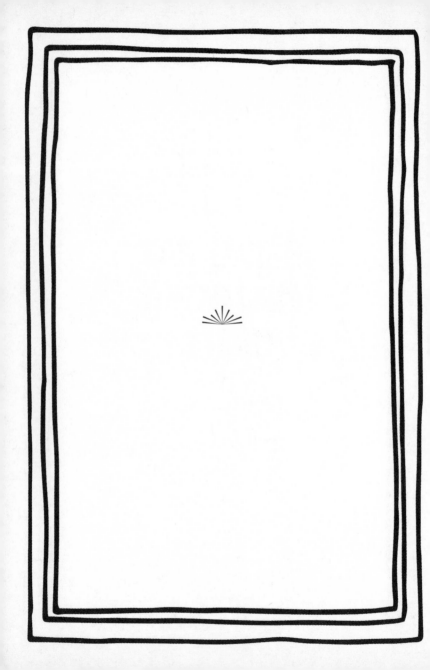

OBVIOUSLY

The clock is running down. Game tied. Thirty precious seconds remaining. Emotions are running at a fever pitch. The coach calls his last time-out and gathers his troops around him, quickly sketches out a diagram on his clipboard, and issues his orders.

They are all professionals — the best of the best. They know the game, inside and out. Collectively, they have well over a hundred years of basketball experience among them.

What could the coach be telling them that they don't already know? Is he speaking in some secret code, unintelligible to mere mortals? I imagined it went something like this: "Okay, listen up. We're going with Zebrahawk 18b, subformation Wounded Slozzer. High torpedo on the low frontier. Slant those aviators and flush the pipes. Got it? Okay, now...*let's do this!*"

For most of my lifetime, it was always an intriguing mystery to me...until they started pinning mics on coaches in the NBA. Finally! I had the chance to hear the sage wisdom that had been eluding me for all those years. And, to my astonishment, here are the types of things they were *actually* saying: "Play defense!" "Move the ball!" "No turnovers!" "Make your shots!"

Seriously? That was *it*?! Well, no shit, Sherlock! What could be more obvious? Hell, if that's all it took, even I — a short,

Jewish psychologist — could be a successful coach in the NBA. (I can just see myself in action: "Be assertive, but not aggressive! Protect your self-esteem! And tell me, what were your feelings when you missed that shot?")

But, after mulling this over for quite some time, I came to a different realization. The game is played at a furious pace. The margin for error is virtually nonexistent. And there are dozens — if not hundreds — of things players have to keep track of and to accomplish, all of which are essential. But what the coach is telling them is *really* essential and needs to stand out above all else. So, it turns out that the sage wisdom the coach bestows is to *narrow things down…*

In times of stress or uncertainty, we sometimes need to be reminded of the obvious: Stick with the basics. Focus on your most important goal. Don't get distracted. Execute one thing at a time.

Got it? Okay, now…*let's do this*!

LIFE LESSON:

THERE ARE MERITS TO JUST STICKING WITH THE BASICS.

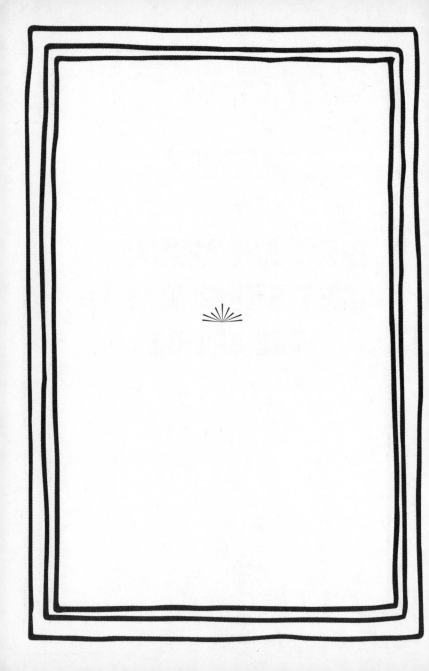

INVERTED SELF-ESTEEM

"What is the *matter* with you, Jerry? How many times do I have to *tell* you these things?!"

I sat timidly outside the office door as Jerry, the neophyte television director, was being raked over the coals by Sid, the crusty, old-school producer.

Sid's voice was coarse and strident: "Can't you do *anything* right?!" Jerry's was faint and timid: "Yes, you're right, Sid. I know I need to do better."

The upbraiding was relentless. "Why don't you ever *listen* to me? You are a *serious* disappointment!" If a tongue lashing could actually pierce flesh, the faded photographs of the has-been TV stars mounted on the wood-paneled office walls would have been splattered with blood.

Jerry was unfailingly repentant: "I am *so* sorry, Sid. Please give me another chance. I can do better."

The rancid concoction of Sid's venomous tirade and Jerry's pitiful responses twisted my stomach into knots. I felt like I personally was on the receiving end of this never-ending barrage. "*Why doesn't Jerry stand up for himself?*" I screamed inside my head. "*This guy's self-esteem must be in the toilet! How much more abuse can poor Jerry bear?*" (Hell, it was almost unbearable for *me*, and I was in the next room!)

I was working as a staff writer for a daytime television series about fictionalized couples in therapy. It was my first professional job as a writer, and I was also in the midst of my doctoral program in psychology. So, it was a fortuitous — if not odd — melding of those two worlds.

Despite my Zorro-esque yearning to leap to Jerry's rescue, I felt absolutely powerless to do anything about it. First, Jerry was an adult and should be able to fend for himself. And second, frankly, I couldn't risk losing my job. But I figured the very least I could do was to offer him my empathy and emotional support. So, I asked him out for an early-morning meal the next day.

Now, some life lessons can only take root with the benefit of decades of hindsight. Others require months. Still others take only weeks. But this one needed less than twenty-four hours. And it happened at a coffee shop counter over a power breakfast of pancakes, sausage, and eggs.

I didn't quite know how to broach the subject. I started with some general chatter about the perils and pitfalls of show biz, the challenges of creativity, and blah, blah, blah. Then I gingerly brought up the topic of Sid. I took a breath. "Jerry, I really feel for you." I sympathetically queried, "How can you stand to listen to his abuse?"

His mouth full of scrambled eggs, he just shrugged it off: "Aw, who bothers to listen?" I kinda sorta laughed, "I can't tell if you're serious." He affirmed, "Of course! I just ignore it. If he wants to get an ulcer, that's up to him. As for me, it doesn't cost me anything. I still have a job. And no ulcer." And with that, he ravenously polished off his pancakes.

Here I thought the poor guy suffered from abysmally low self-esteem. But I was wrong. In fact, his self-esteem was so healthy — so solid — that he was impervious to the rabid onslaughts of a bellicose, infantile bully…who, I realized in that moment, was actually the one with the low self-esteem issues.

Jerry sopped up the last nub of his sausage with a puddle of maple syrup, and we headed back to the office where it all had started. But I had newfound admiration — even envy — toward Jerry. And with it, a new perspective for learning how to cope with some of the Sids in this world.

LIFE LESSON:

HAVE THE WISDOM NOT TO FIGHT EVERY BATTLE.

WHEN INTUITION GOES AWRY

☞ "Don't trust your senses."

☞ "Don't follow your gut feeling."

☞ "Don't believe your intuition."

Who would proffer such cynical decrees? Some frothy-lipped curmudgeon, emphatically pounding a wooden cane on his rickety front porch, rivulets of spittle oozing down his stubbly chin?

Hardly. These were the words of pilots. Navy pilots. Navy *fighter* pilots.

One rainy Sunday afternoon, I sat glued to The History Channel (back when The History Channel used to broadcast actual documentaries about actual history — rather than serving up pseudo-documentary fare like "UFO Hunters, "Nostradamus Effect," and "Ancient Aliens"), binge watching a series on military aircraft. I was especially intrigued by interviews with Navy jet fighter pilots, who described in exhilarating and terrifying detail the perils of their occupation.

And what did they frequently report being their most harrowing experiences? Battling enemy fighters in high-speed, air-to-air combat? No, actually in *peace time* — when landing on an aircraft carrier at night in bad weather. Why? Because under these circumstances, their senses can easily deceive them. Their gut feelings could lead them astray. Their intuitive hunches might prove to be disastrous. In short, when they trust only what they see with their own eyes, they risk a catastrophic crash and burn.

What, instead, should they rely on? Their instruments. When they trust what their cockpit gauges tell them, then they are more likely to land safely. Through rigorous training and by sheer force of will, they learn to override their own instincts — *even though "it feels so wrong."*

I later came to realize that "instruments" needn't refer just to navigational aids or other measurement devices. It can, more generally, mean any objective information we use for guidance — from reading an instruction manual, to evaluating data for financial investments, to determining whether or not someone is worthy of your trust.

Case in point: Have you ever "fallen in love"…with the wrong person? I certainly have (and, embarrassingly, more than once). You might acknowledge to yourself that, yes, they are rather emotionally unstable. And okay, their behavior might be irresponsibly impulsive. And sure, they might have a history littered with stormy interpersonal relationships. And granted, they frequently drink too much alcohol.

"But," you assure yourself, "our connection feels so deep! How could something that feels this right possibly be wrong?" Your entrusted friends and family may even try to warn you away. "No, this time will be different," you try to convince them (and yourself). But of course, it won't be. Just like the Navy fighter pilot, when you don't trust the information — your "instruments" — you risk a catastrophic crash and burn — *even though "it feels so right."*

Now, I'm not saying that we should *never* trust our intuition, instincts, or gut feelings. They can be extraordinary and sometimes miraculous conduits to creative inspiration, aesthetic appreciation, emotional truth, and a richness of human experience. Moreover, we want to believe in their power — they make us feel special and somehow connected to a force of universal wisdom.

But *feelings aren't facts*. And whether or not we like to admit it, they can cloud our judgment and lead us astray. (Did you ever have the "gut feeling" to kick somebody right in the gut?) We tend to remember when they were right, but not when they were wrong. We disregard data at our own peril.

It's a matter of keeping it all in balance — pay attention to your intuitive feelings, but have some trust in your instruments. In short, intuition is usually the first word, and sometimes the last word, but should never be the only word. But don't take my word for it…you can take it up with the United States Navy.

LIFE LESSON:

LEARN WHEN TO TRUST FACTS OVER FEELINGS.

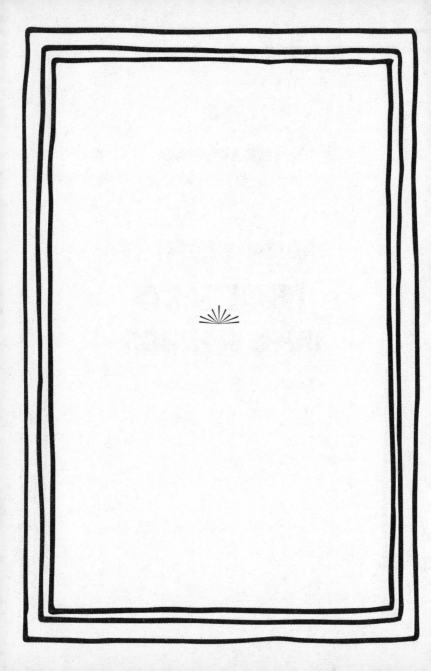

THE PROZAC DILEMMA

So it had come down to this: A little paper cup and a green-and-yellow pill. I stood at the drinking fountain of the UCLA student health clinic, staring down at the innocuous yet ominous capsule resting in the palm of my hand.

The year was 1988, and the medication — Prozac — was being trumpeted as a revolutionary breakthrough in the treatment of depression. I had been wrestling with what Winston Churchill called "The Black Dog" periodically throughout my life. But this was a particularly nasty bout, one which I just couldn't seem to shake. Believe me when I tell you that I tried every reasonable remedy — therapy, exercise, social support, meditation, and more…but with one exception: I had stubbornly rejected trying any kind of medication.

My concerns were numerous: What if I become dependent on the drugs? What if I get side effects? Could I bear the stigma of relying on pills? Shouldn't the chemistry in my brain be off-limits to alteration? Shouldn't I be able to solve this problem on my own, without resorting to medication (especially since I was becoming a *psychologist*, for God's sake)? And maybe most frightening of all, what if the medicine changes "who I am?"

For each concern, however, I had a rational counterpoint. I knew that these types of medications aren't addictive, so my becoming dependent was unlikely. As far as experiencing side effects, I could just discontinue the pills. And by that point, I was feeling so rotten, I didn't really much care about stigma or what other people might think. Plus, I knew logically that there was nothing holy about neurotransmitters, since it's all just physiology anyway. And finally, I had already attempted — unsuccessfully — to solve it "on my own." But all of this notwithstanding, I was still reluctant to cross the Pharmaceutical Rubicon.

As I pondered this dilemma, it became apparent to me that I was not going to stumble across any clear, simple answer — because there was no escaping the truism that *every* decision or event in life involves some kind of trade-off. For everything we gain, we always give something up. Likewise, for everything we lose, there is some potential upside. If you gain a relationship, you trade off some independence. If you quit your job, you gain the prospect of new opportunity. But we can't have it both ways: Whatever choice you make leaves all others behind. If you turn left, you give up turning right. If you eat your cake, you can't then have it too. For any decision, the best we can do is to weigh out the costs and benefits, then go with the one where the balance is tipped.

And in this case, the cost involved a very specific type of risk. For years, I was afraid that taking medication would change "who I am." But in that moment, I was faced with an even bigger fear: Now, I was afraid that it *wouldn't*. I viewed medication as my option of last resort — something I could turn to if all else failed. And there was some comfort, even security, in knowing that I carried that option in my back pocket. But what if I tried it — and it didn't work? I'd then be left empty, with no backup solutions at all. And that prospect was terrifying.

Unpredictable risks can be gut-wrenching. What if you decide to make a major career change only to find out later that it made no real difference in your life? What happens if you lose a massive amount of weight, or even undergo cosmetic surgery, and you don't feel any better about yourself? What if you quit drinking alcohol only to find that you've only replaced one set of problems with another? What if you end your relationship and still feel miserable — or even *more* miserable?

Deciding about change is a matter of weighing risks. Do you risk failure by changing? Or do you risk remaining stuck by *not* changing? One useful tool I've found is to imagine yourself sometime in the future, looking back at the decision you're facing. How do you think you might feel about yourself if you took the risk to change? And how about if you took the risk not to change?

But that thought experiment aside, how do we find out if we made a good choice? Truth be told: By actually finding out.

So, I did. From the palm of my hand and into my mouth, down went the pill. For better or for worse, I opted to take the plunge. How did it work out? Unfortunately, I had to discontinue the meds due to their side effects. But I don't view the decision as a failure. In hindsight, I'm still glad that I took that risk of trying; for me, finding out was worth the trade-off.

LIFE LESSON:

EVERY DECISION
INVOLVES TRADE-OFFS.

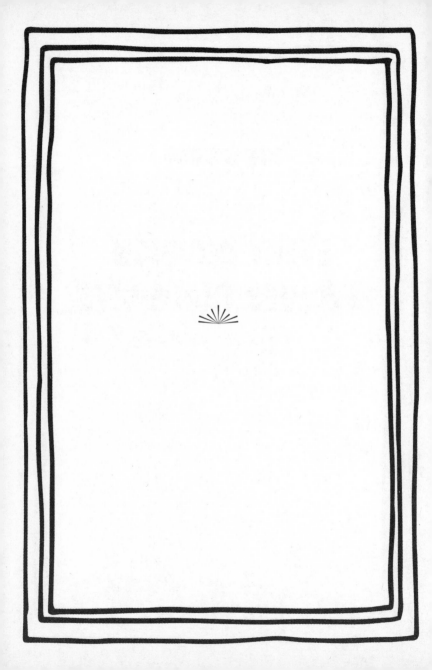

PSEUDO-WORRIES

Paralyzed with indecisiveness, I gazed into the mirror. "What color shirt should I wear for the job interview tomorrow morning — the light blue or the light gray?" I'd try one on, then the other, and then back again. Reaching a final verdict seemed an insurmountable feat. I had once read somewhere that blue represents loyalty, serenity, and calmness. On the other hand, gray is supposed to reflect stability, maturity, and balance. What kind of "statement" did I want to convey? Which choice might give me a psychological edge? It was as if the entire weight of the interview — not to mention my professional career — hinged entirely on an arbitrary textile shade.

Even while I was spinning out on the OCD Hamster Wheel, I knew it was crazy. I kept repeating to myself, "Quit wasting all of your time and energy on this!" But to no avail. Of course, I understood full well that the hue of my shirt wasn't going to make any difference; what really counted was my professional resume and how I handled myself the next morning. But, the night before the interview, there was nothing I could do about either of those. All I had was a bundle of anxiety…and the ability to decide on a shirt color.

In a manner of speaking, fretting about my shirt was a "little worry" — because the logical part of my brain knew that *it didn't really matter.* In contrast, "big worries" concern things that actually are important, but we can rarely do much — if anything — about. Like what happens in the stock market. Or like getting blindsided on the highway. Or watching your elderly parents become increasingly frail. Or even events as mundane as the outcome of a football game or a change in the weather. On the other hand, what about deciding whether to have your eggs scrambled or poached? Or how often to scrub your kitchen floor? Or what color shirt to wear? Now, *those* you can control.

It dawned on me that, in a sense, "little worries" are actually *easy worries:* It's easier to obsess over the trivial things that are controllable because it spares us from obsessing over big things that aren't. *Aha!* So, there actually was some functional value to my neurotic worry! Of course, attaining that insight didn't stop me from doing it — but it did help to dial things back a bit. And, as an added benefit, my whole mental jitterbug became rather amusing to observe.

I don't remember which shirt I ended up selecting. I don't remember if I got the job. In fact, I don't even remember what the interview was for. But this much I do remember: The color of my shirt had absolutely no impact whatsoever on the outcome.

I'm not saying to "simply stop worrying" about the trivial stuff. (That advice is much easier said than done.) As a matter of fact, if worrying about the small stuff distracts or protects you from worrying about the big stuff, then try to take some solace in the worry itself. Just realize why you're doing it; then you can go back to obsessing about eggs, kitchen floors, and shirt colors.

And for those of us who might even be afraid of giving up some worries out of fear that we'll be left somehow more vulnerable to bad things that can befall us, here's my advice: *Don't worry!* There will always be something else to worry about…

LIFE LESSON:

IT'S EASIER TO WORRY ABOUT THINGS WE CAN CONTROL THAN THINGS WE CAN'T.

"HE JUST DOESN'T UNDERSTAND"

She had turned over every stone. Or so she ardently believed. "Honey, you need to get a job," her husband repeatedly insisted, with metronomic regularity. "We've got two kids, and we can't make it on my income alone." "I can't take it anymore!" she beseeched me one summer afternoon. "He just won't budge! He doesn't get it! He just keeps telling me the same thing, over and over!" By this point, she had worked herself into a lather. I took a deep breath. "Well, how do you usually respond?" I softly inquired, doing my best to remain calm and neutral. After all, these were my neighbors and I didn't want to risk alienating either of them. Her reply was swift, loud, and shrill: "I've tried *everything!* I tried crying, I tried yelling, I tried the silent treatment. *Nothing worked!*"

I felt my pulse quicken, my cheeks flush, and my head starting to spin. My self-imposed veil of neutrality was now on the verge of unraveling. She must have seen my eyes darting back and forth, futilely searching for something approaching a non-offensive solution. "Seriously?! Nothing worked? You've tried *everything*? *Have you tried getting a freakin' job*?!" But of course, I didn't actually utter any of those words. I finally semi-mumbled the phrase, "Sounds really frustrating." She nodded briefly and continued to whine relentlessly about her unjust plight.

Was I being cowardly? Wise? Empathic? Dense? After all these years, I'm still not certain. But one thing I am certain of: She wasn't really interested in an answer...at least not my answer.

LIFE LESSON:

'TIS BETTER TO SOLVE
THAN TO COMPLAIN.

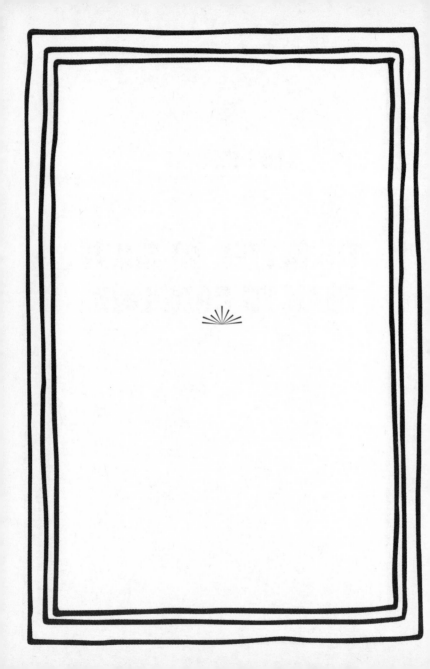

LYING OR CRAZY?

Come on now, tell the truth: You don't *actually* like the taste of raw oysters, do you? I'm talkin' no lemon, no cocktail sauce, no horseradish, no Tabasco, no nothing…just those cold, slimy, gray, elephant loogies.

And what about so-called "free jazz?" You don't know what I'm referring to? Well, free jazz almost defies verbal definition, but, unlike traditional jazz composition, is marked by the abandonment of preset chord progressions, a lack of melodic patterns, and often involves the technique of "overblowing" one's instrument. Still not clear? Okay, check out a couple selections on YouTube. Go ahead, I'll wait… Well, what do you think? Am I right, or am I right? Now, I ask you: Since when did cacophonous, grating, random notes qualify for "jazz" — let alone "music"?

Clearly, I don't like raw oysters or free jazz. But just as clearly, others do. And here's the rub: It can be difficult — sometimes impossible — to believe that other people genuinely like something that you don't (and vice versa) because their perceptions are so alien to our personal tastes.

Let's grant that some people *claim* to like things that they actually don't, simply because they enjoy being nonconforming, contrarian, or cheeky. (For these self-styled rebels, the very notion of not being seen as "cool," "hip," or at least "unconventional" would cause their very identity to evaporate.) But that still leaves a whole group of other people who are being neither untruthful nor disingenuous; yet accepting their viewpoint as valid can be challenging.

Strongly held differences between people are understandable when debating emotionally laden subjects, like politics or religion. But the same principle holds true even when we're talking about relatively mundane or trivial things, like fashion, sports, or even the weather.

This point was driven home to me one afternoon as I commenced a lecture to my class of psychology students. After I finished taking roll, I crumpled up a piece of paper and then launched it toward the waste basket…which, of course, I missed. I brushed off the flubbed shot with some self-disparaging remark ("People occasionally don't mistake me for Michael Jordan"), my students chuckled at their bungling professor, and I proceeded with the lecture. But I noticed that a sense of distress began to creep across the class — or, more specifically, *part* of the class: Some students were starting to squirm, glancing at the wad of paper lying on the floor, then back at me, and then back at the paper. The collective look on their faces said it all: "*Is this guy going to pick that thing up or not?!*" At the same time, I observed that other students didn't seem to care — or even to notice. So, as a semi-scientific/semi-sadistic social experiment, I just continued my lecture, all the while totally ignoring the crumpled wad.

After a few very long minutes, I seized the moment as a teaching opportunity: "I'm curious…please raise your hand if that piece of paper is bothering you." The hands of about half the class urgently shot up toward the heavens, expressing relief that I had finally addressed the five hundred-pound gorilla (well, tiny wad of paper) in the room. I continued, "Now, raise your hand if it *doesn't* bother you." The rest of the students looked around with a shrug, not quite understanding why this was even an issue, and slowly raised their hands.

I queried the class, "So, how do you explain the fact that some of the other students reacted so differently than you?" Someone immediately blurted out, "Well, either they're lying or they're crazy!" Of course, it got a laugh. But the comment was illuminating.

"Okay," I began, "for those of you who aren't bothered by that piece of paper, it's probably *inconceivable* to you that it actually could be a source of agony to others, right? But here's the thing: It genuinely is. And, for those of you whom it *does* bother, it is similarly unimaginable that the paper doesn't matter in the least to others. Yet, it truly doesn't. This might even call into question the honesty of those who have a different response than yours, but remember, just like the Rorschach inkblot test — people really do have different perceptions about the same thing."

I'm sure my students understood this simple idea. However, it turns out to be a bit more complicated than that. Over the years, I have noticed that some people feel uncomfortable, annoyed, or even belligerent when others express their differences: "What do you *mean* you don't eat meat?! Just have some!" "You don't want to have children? What's the *matter* with you?!" "You're not drinking alcohol? What's your problem? Come on, get with it and join the party!"

This always struck me as not only irrational, but also rather odd. After all, what business is it of theirs? Why should it matter to them if someone else elects not to eat meat, have kids, drink, or any other myriad choices? But it started to make some sense to me when I realized that these individuals somehow perceive the differences as a *threat* — to their views, to their values, even to their identity. In other words, due to their own insecurities, they take other people's beliefs *personally*. And when that happens, they get defensive, needing to push back and persuade — or even coerce — others to conform with them. But *differentness, in itself, is not a threat.*

Conversely, when people are more emotionally secure, they view differences with others with acceptance, interest, or even as an opportunity to learn and to grow. At least, that's how I aspire to live my life now and in the future…except when it comes to raw oysters and free jazz…I can only pray that I will *never* be that "evolved."

(P.S. Also, while you're on YouTube, check out "Yanny vs. Laurel" — and anybody who hears "Laurel" is either lying or crazy…)

LIFE LESSON:

DIFFERENTNESS IN ITSELF IS NOT A THREAT.

"WE HOLD THESE TRUTHS..."

Once they morph into miserable teenagers, it's inconceivable that they actually used to be innocent, fun, and loving children. One morning, over a kids' "power breakfast" — frozen waffles and chocolate milk — I queried my four-year-old son, Jacob, on some of his thoughts about his family.

Why do you love Auntie Carrie?

Because she plays with me.

Why do you love Uncle Robert?

Because he takes me on his boat.

Why do you love Auntie LuJean?

Because she takes care of me.

Why do you love Uncle Michael?

Because he takes me for rides.

Why do you love your cousins, Rachel, Rosie, Allegra, Hannah, and Dana?

Because they are beautiful.

Why do you love grandpa?

Because he makes me laugh.

Why do you love grandma?

Because she gives me desserts.

Why do you love mommy?

Because she makes me tacos.

Why do you love daddy?

(after a brief pause) *Because I just do.*

In Junior High School, I learned that some truths are self-evident, like the right to Life, Liberty, and the pursuit of Happiness. But it wasn't until many years later that I learned first-hand that there was one more self-evident truth, just as important: love.

LIFE LESSON:

LOVE IS A SELF-EVIDENT TRUTH.

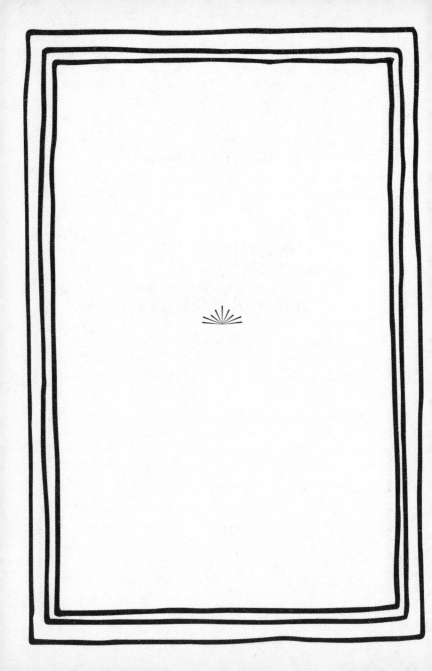

BIOFEEDBACK

"Ooo, look Daddy! Bunny!" My two-year-old daughter, Briana, was frenetically pointing, bouncing, and squealing with delight. We were plopped on the couch early one Sunday morning, channel surfing through the too-many options available on cable TV. Sure enough, there was the most adorable little rabbit, hippity-hopping across a meadow. We settled in, just Daddy and Be-Bop (my nickname for her), to relish the spectacle of the delightful furry creature. But no sooner had I placed the remote control down beside me, when the camera panned back to reveal that the frolicking bunny was, in fact, being feverishly pursued by a bloodthirsty fox. Recognizing that catastrophe was imminent, I made a mad reach for the remote, fumbling it in my hands (like Fredo Corleone's gun in *The Godfather*). But alas, too late. The doomed bunny's fate was sealed. We watched on in silent horror as it was dragged mercilessly to the ground.

I felt consumed by empathy and guilt. I had failed to protect my innocent daughter from the cruel brutality of nature. Be-Bop's eyes welled with anguish and tears. "Daddy, I don't like this," she softly whimpered. I was at a loss for words. What's a parent supposed to offer at a time like this? Some inane fatherly lecture about "the cycle of life?" Though I tried to act calm, my soul ached. All I could eke out was a feeble, "How come, sweetheart?" Her response was simple: "Because it makes my throat dry and my stomach hurt." (Definitely *not* the answer I was expecting.)

It wasn't "I'm sad." Or, "I'm scared for the bunny." Or even, "I'm mad at the fox." Nothing like that. No, she actually was answering my question in the most plain and direct way possible. She didn't like it because it made her physically feel bad. She didn't need the label of any particular emotion; the raw physiological sensation was enough to let her know how she felt — which was *bad*.

In an odd way, it reminded me of how our family dog, Zorro, would pick out his toys to play with. He'd ritually drag out a wicker basket loaded with doggie playthings, then methodically remove them, one at a time. If his verdict was thumbs down (or, I guess, "paws down"), he'd toss it aside. Rubber ring? Nope. Plastic ball? Nah. Pull rope? Negatory. The rite would continue until he came across the one that evidently suited his preference. Squeaky piglet? Aha! That's the one! Then off he would prance, toy-in-mouth, for hours of bow-wow delight. And each day brought a different choice.

I'd wonder, *what on earth was the basis of his selection?* After all, it's just a random assortment of doggie toys, all of which, at different times, he enjoyed playing with. I could only assume that as he was rummaging through his playthings, he was awaiting some kind of inner "*Ding!*" that prompted his decision.

He wasn't searching simply for a toy; he was searching for a particular *feeling* — a cue that let him know that *this* was the "right" toy.

We are all like Zorro. And Briana. How do we conclude if we like or dislike a type of food? Or clothing fashion? Or piece of art? Or music? It starts with a gut feeling (a visceral "*yeah!*" or "*yech!*") that our body conveys to us if it's pleasant or unpleasant.

Same goes for dating choices. Typically, one is looking for "chemistry," right? But it's less about the social chemistry between you and someone else, and more about the actual chemistry within yourself. Like a flutter in your chest. Or a racing pulse. Or a warm glow. Or a certain tingly feeling. "We had chemistry" really means "I felt chemistry." Likewise, what if you're left feeling kind of numb? Or drained? Or empty? Or bored? In that instance, "we didn't have any chemistry" equates to "I felt no chemistry."

So, how did things turn out with my distraught daughter on that fateful Sunday morning? Fortunately, I was able to salvage the debacle by trying a different tack: "Be-Bop, how about a big scoop of Haagen-Dazs coffee ice cream covered with sliced bananas and chocolate syrup on a toasted waffle?" Within moments, her body transported her from anguish to ecstasy. Her eyes widened, and she was licking her lips in anticipatory delight. I had my answer…and she didn't need to utter a single word.

Want to know what you're feeling about something — or someone? It's a good idea to start by listening to what your body is trying to tell you. The question, "how are you feeling?" isn't an intellectual endeavor; it's literally, "how are you *feeling*?"

YOUR BODY IS THE CONDUIT TO YOUR EMOTIONS.

JOURNEY B. GOODE

It could never come soon enough. "It" was a lot of things. My birthday. A trip. A concert. The first day of daylight saving's time. Anything I was looking forward to.

But lamentably enough, no matter how good "it" was, it was invariably anti-climactic. I mean, after all that anticipation, it could never hope to live up to expectations. How could there not be some kind of letdown? There was just too much damn pressure on the event. The long stretches of waiting were just something to be not-so-patiently endured.

Such was the pattern throughout the first half-century of my life. But then, tickets to a Chuck Berry concert turned it all around.

I had always been a zealous fan of the rock 'n' roll icon, and the few times in my youth when I saw him perform were both electrifying and mesmerizing. So, years later when I became a parent, I was hell-bent on ensuring that my kids would have the opportunity to experience his musical magnificence. I relished the fantasy that, one day in the distant future — long after I'm dead and buried — they could proudly boast to their grandchildren: "Chuck Berry? Sure, I know who Chuck Berry was. In fact, I actually saw him perform. *Live.*"

Of course, by the time my kids were old enough to see him, he was well into his eighties, and certainly not the impossibly vibrant force he once was. But, come on…it was still *Chuck Friggin' Berry*. I knew I'd always regret it if I passed up the chance.

And then chance found me one summer evening, when I heard on AM radio that he was scheduled to perform a single show in the early fall at a very small venue at the Route 66 classic auto show in the Southern California desert community of San Bernardino. Without a nanosecond of hesitation, I jumped on the internet and scored second-row seats.

And literally every day thereafter, whether on my hike, my bicycle, or in my car, I'd crank up my iPod with his classics: "Johnny B. Goode," "Rock and Roll Music," "Maybellene," "Back in the USA." I'd share the building anticipation with my friends. We wondered, what songs would he play? Would he do his legendary "duck walk?" How many of those signature musical licks — the ones he invented over half a century ago to create the original sound of rock and roll guitar — would I be privileged to hear?

The day before the concert, I was on my bike ride, rockin' and rollin' to "Roll Over Beethoven." And I was happy. I mean, *really happy*. But seemingly out of nowhere, a weird, cold feeling crept into the pit of my stomach, sunk my shoulders, and furrowed my brow: "Oh, shit. What if he's not any good? What if Grandfather

Time has reduced him to just an empty shell of what he once was? What if my kids resent me for dragging them out to the desert just to see some old guy on stage trying pathetically to act cool? What if the whole thing is an enormous bust??"

Then it struck me: *It didn't really matter how the concert turned out.* Or whether or not he was any good. I'd just had three months of joyful anticipation. The concert itself was almost an afterthought. Sure, I still hoped he'd be great. But somehow it wasn't the be-all-end-all. The buildup — rather than being a source of potential disappointment — was actually the joy.

As it turned out, the concert itself was a great experience. On some songs he faltered. On some songs he shined. I got to watch my daughter Briana beam as Chuck seemed to sing a verse of "School Days" right to her. I saw my son Jacob transfixed as Chuck made his Gibson guitar warble and whine. *My kids got to see Chuck Berry perform live.*

But as gratified as I was by all of this, what I took away was a lesson that had always maintained cliché status throughout my life, until I personally experienced it to be true: It's less about the destination and more about the journey.

When I was younger, "it" could never come soon enough. But now, it always seems to come too soon. So, *don't rush it.*

P. S. I just purchased concert tickets to hear Beethoven's Ninth symphony performed at Disney Concert Hall. The concert isn't for another six months…and for that I am grateful. I now have half a year ahead of joyful anticipation. Now, off for a hike. iPod fully locked and loaded. Roll Over Beethoven!

THE JOURNEY CAN BE MORE SATISFYING THAN THE DESTINATION.

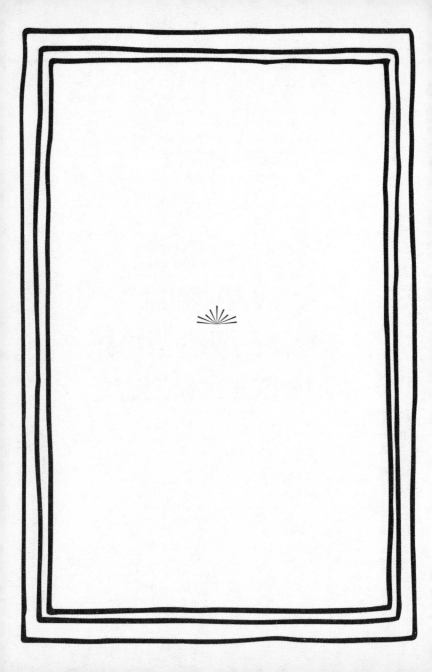

TO LOVE, HONOR, AND BETRAY

Those who don't know the value of loyalty, can never appreciate the cost of betrayal.

— Unknown

Divorce is never pretty, and usually downright ugly. Things that you once held to be true become both inverted and shredded. The one person in the world in whom you had placed your unconditional trust has now transmuted into the one person in the world you trust the least. Your once-protective firewall of loyalty has been reduced to a heap of smoldering rubble.

Lies. Deceit. Vindictiveness. They're all part of the whole unholy cavalcade of horror. The well-being of children, emotional health, and financial security — all thrown into chaos.

The ache was so deep it is nearly indescribable. Waking up in the middle of the night to the sounds of myself gasping for air. Walking through the day like the living dead, not even able to recall what it was like to feel human. Desperately searching for any true thing to cling to. Scraped so raw inside, I wondered why I hadn't bled through to my skin.

It's a time when one's family and friends become invaluable reservoirs of support, validation, and hope. I knew I could lean on them until I learned to breathe again. And, fortunately for me, they all instinctively rushed to my side to offer whatever they could…with only one exception: my friend Gino.

Gino and I had been the best of friends. Over the course of more than forty years, we traveled together, confided in each other, debated politics with each other, and stood up with each other at our weddings. No one was more trustworthy and loyal. Until…

For reasons that are still baffling to me, Gino suddenly felt the need to assume a stance of neutrality, refusing "to take sides" — as if he were Switzerland in the midst of the German Third Reich's savage march through Europe. In divorce, the courts are obligated to be neutral. But with family and friends, there is no Switzerland. Choosing "neutrality" is, in fact, choosing a side. And in this case, it wasn't with his friend. It's one thing to be serially betrayed by a spouse. But a best friend? "*Et tu, Gino?*"

For me, this was confusing at best, and deeply disturbing at worst. I implored him to understand, but he just dug ever deeper into his Swiss bedrock. And when he disdainfully scolded me for "not showing enough empathy" during the divorce proceedings, he evidently didn't see the hypocritical irony. Mutual friends we shared for decades were all shocked by his behavior: "Gino!? But he's the most loyal guy in the world! What's the *matter* with him?"

And so it went, month after miserable month. When I tried to explain how painful this was to me, he pushed back with defensiveness, arguments, and rationalizations. He simply refused to budge — or display any hint of understanding.

Then one day he called our mutual friend, Mare, to see how I was doing. "David isn't upset with me or anything, is he?" he asked innocently. Mare's response was measured but direct: "He most certainly is, Gino! David is your best friend! And you are not being a good friend to him!" Taken aback, he asked her what she meant. Mare then went through, point by point, the multiple ways he had profoundly let me down. If he had been clueless over the previous several months, he certainly couldn't be now.

Gino's response seemed so heartfelt: "Oh, I see what you mean! Man, that's *terrible*. I don't *ever* want to jeopardize my friendship with David. I'm gonna call him right away!" Mare hung up the phone, and contacted me immediately, delighted to share the good news: Gino understood. And I should expect a call from him.

Days passed…and then a week…as I anxiously waited for the call that never came. Mare checked in to see if I'd heard from him. "Not a word," I regretfully informed her. After a long pause, Mare uttered the words of wisdom that seemed to capture it all: "Gino isn't the man he thinks he is."

Gino always prided himself as overflowing with compassion and empathy, unfailingly able to "see all sides" in a conflict. As a self-proclaimed socialist, he especially saw himself as a champion of the world's downtrodden, ready to stand up and fight for unfairness, injustice, and anyone who has been wronged. Anyone, evidently, except his best friend.

Being betrayed at the same time by both your spouse and your closest friend fractures the foundation of one's deepest beliefs. It is a profoundly disorienting experience to discover that people can change in ways you could never imagine. You think you know somebody — then you don't. It's enough to make you feel that you'll never be able to trust again…

And what is to be learned from all of this unrelenting disillusionment? Unfortunately, the life lesson from this story is neither clear nor simple. "Shit happens?" Too obvious. "Never trust anyone except your dog?" Too cynical. "The best laid plan of mice and men often go awry?" Already been done.

No, for me, it's more about emerging with a greater sense of gratitude for what you do have, not just the painful loss of what you don't have — gratitude for friends, family, pets, and other loving relationships that have yet to be discovered. Oh, and there's one more upside: Once you've survived all of that emotional anguish, life can't help but become *much* brighter afterward.

When the chips are high, everybody wants to be your friend. When the chips are low, you find out who your friends are. But when the chips are gone, you find out who your *real* friends are. And to this day, I feel blessed that I have so many of them... albeit minus one.

THE EXPERIENCE OF BETRAYAL ACCENTUATES THE VALUE OF LOYALTY.

ZORRO GOES HOME

Zorro was 120 pounds of massive black Labrador love. Big floppy ears. Warm brown eyes. An absolutely gigantic cranium. Jaws that could easily crush a human hand, yet such a thought would never dare enter his gentle soul. I know, everyone's dog is the best dog who ever lived…but mine seriously *was*.

If you've never experienced the heart-melting euphoria of beholding a litter of squirming, squealing Labrador puppies (or really, any puppies for that matter) …well, you should try it sometime. It will restore your faith in goodness.

Out of the gang of pups, we instantly knew which was destined to be The One. We didn't even have to pick him out; fact is, he picked *us* out. Scampering his way over the other puppies and wagging his tiny tail, he homed in on my five-year-old son — enthusiastically smothering Jacob's face with licks, kisses, and love. We named him "Zorro" — after my childhood hero, the dashing figure who cloaked himself in black and gallantly protected all those in need.

From the moment we brought him home, Zorro was a nonstop source of unbridled enjoyment. As a puppy, he would sprint across the kitchen floor, realizing only too late that he was unable to put on his doggie brakes; he'd then frantically back pedal, his ridiculously large paws getting no traction — like a character in an old Warner Brothers cartoon — and crash headlong into the cabinet…yet he'd just shake it off and emerge unscathed and ready for more playtime.

Sure, puppyhood can be a pain in any family's collective butt… but it still passes much too quickly. As Zorro entered adolescence, his little puppy yap transformed into a not insignificant canine *woof!* We spent countless hours playing fetch in the backyard, hiking in the Santa Monica Mountains, and taking day trips to the lake where he'd repeatedly dive into the chilly waters — paddling frenetically and using his Labrador tail as a rudder — to retrieve the rubber toy that we kept tossing in. But perhaps our favorite activity was taking long walks in the neighborhood, with my daughter (and Zorro's adopted sister) Briana. In order to train him where to go if he ever got lost, we'd finish our walk with, "Home! We're going home!" Zorro would always brighten up, and bolt back toward our house, dragging us by his leash.

He was a trusted companion and emotional protector for twelve years — through good times and bad: When we brought Briana home as a newborn, as my kids matured through childhood, throughout Jacob's school years, when our house was torn apart during its remodeling, during my separation and divorce. Through it all, Zorro was always there. Ever playful. Ever loyal. Ever loving. Ever happy just being in his family's presence.

But time passes and spares no one…not even Zorro the Lab. It started innocently enough, with some white fur making its appearance around his muzzle and his gait gradually slowing down. But then his rear legs started to give way, and it became harder and harder for him to walk. When he'd stumble to the ground, he looked up at me, confused, hoping I'd be able to help him, or at least to be understanding: He was doing his best.

I didn't anticipate that my visit with him to the vet that November afternoon was going to be our last. After a careful examination, the vet's face looked kind but sober. Then she said in words what her expression had already communicated: "I think his time has come. But it's up to you." *Up to me?* The very thought was unthinkable. What a heavy burden and humbling responsibility. I pleaded with myself, couldn't I have just one more week — even one more day — with him? Or was I being selfish trying to keep him alive so I wouldn't have to lose him? But I knew he wasn't having fun anymore. And he was more than uncomfortable — he was hurting. Zorro trusted me implicitly. During his lifetime, he sometimes needed me to help him when he couldn't help himself. And now, he needed me in a way that he never did before…to help him end his suffering.

The vet told me I could take all the time I needed, and then left us alone. I sat on the cold tile floor, cradling Zorro's weighty head in my arms, stroking his weakened body. I didn't know what to say…and then I did. I gently and reassuringly spoke to him, the memories flooding back:

Remember when we first brought you home, how you'd paw your way across our faces, showering us with your puppy breath?

Remember how you'd chew everything in sight? Furniture, shoes, even garbage?

Remember the time you cornered a possum in the yard…and then looked back at me, with no idea what was supposed to happen next?

Remember the time you broke into a big bin of dog food and ate yourself nearly into a puppy coma?

Remember how you'd nudge me with your rope and demand that I play tug of war with you — until my arms were nearly dislocated from my sockets?

Remember how you'd eat branches of bamboo, and then later you'd sheepishly approach me — to unceremoniously pull them out of your rear end?

Remember how our neighbor's Jack Russell terrier would burrow under their wooden fence, dart across the street, and then wait patiently on our porch for the chance to play with you, his canine pal?

Remember how you would wake yourself up with a startle from the sound of your own snoring…and sometimes your own farts?

Remember how you'd fall asleep next to everyone in the den, feeling safe and secure with your adopted pack?

There was more I needed to say:

I'm sorry I didn't spend more time with you.

I'm sorry I didn't take you on more walks.

I'm sorry if you ever felt ignored.

Please forgive me.

I love you, Zorro.

The time had come. I kissed him gently on the snout. The vet came in to release Zorro from his anguish. Wait…there was one more thing I could say to him that might bring him some peace and comfort in his final moments on earth:

Home. Zorro, we're going home. We're going home…

If he could have smiled, I'm certain he would have. He gently closed his big brown eyes for the last time. His body was still warm…but he was gone. The vet left us alone again. I just clung to him, nuzzling him with my face. Then it was time for me to go home. But this time, alone, in an empty car, without my beloved companion…

All these years later, I still miss the presence of my trusted friend, adopted family member, and heroic protector. But I rest comfortably, knowing that I loved him enough not to selfishly hang on to him; but instead, to let him go. And to set him free. Zorro was, at long last, home.

LIFE LESSON:

LOVE SOMETHING ENOUGH TO LET IT GO.

PERFECTLY FLAWED

Some call me "anal retentive." Others refer to me as "OCD." Still others might describe me as exacting, finicky, rigid, or perfectionistic.

Diagnostic labels aside, I must admit that I've got a little bit of all those qualities. Okay, perhaps a little more than "a little." (All right, so maybe a lot more than "a little.") I'll put it another way: My middle initial, "A," does not stand for "Any-Way-The-Wind-Blows."

But truth be told, I'm kind of proud of that. If I take on a task, it is absolutely inconceivable for me not to doggedly see it through to completion. I enjoy being meticulously organized. The items on my desk all are delightfully arranged at perpendicular angles. The frames in my home are never — and I mean *never* — askew. Even the tools displayed on the pegboard in my garage are positioned with an aesthetic flair. (Mind you, owing to my cultural heritage, I have no idea how to actually *use* most of these tools...but they do look really cool.)

However, there is a cost to all of this: It's a lot of work. Perfectionism requires eternal vigilance and unremitting maintenance. When things "aren't right," it's mentally burdensome. And when newly acquired possessions become scraped, scratched, dinged, dented, or otherwise damaged, it really can be a source of distress…at least it *used* to be.

I spent much of my life constantly worrying about even minor imperfections to my stuff. Even as a kid, I'd safeguard my album covers by encasing them in plastic sleeves and stowing them safely on my closet shelf. I would obsessively polish the chrome on my Schwinn bicycle to eradicate any onset of rusty pitting. Into adulthood, scuffs on my shoes, blemishes on my clothes, and road splats on my car needed immediate attention and remedy.

I lived in a state of perpetual apprehension about that inescapable first flaw. But over the years — and having survived some pretty calamitous life experiences — something changed. The dread of imperfection has given way to acceptance of its inevitability. Rather than dreading the first flaw, now I almost welcome the relief it provides — once it occurs, I never have to worry about it again…

Now, I'm not saying that I *love* it. And of course, I don't go out of my way to cause damage to my stuff. (I may be neurotic, but I'm not crazy!) Plus I must confess, I do still get a certain buzz from beholding the unblemished perfection of a pristine new item, right out of the box.

But "perfection" has been redefined. If it's accompanied by worry, it's not all that perfect. Now I view defect-free stuff as just waiting to experience some life.

With all that said, everything has its limits…Although I'm glad that I've found freedom in imperfection, some things don't change: I'm still compelled to finish my tasks, to organize my schedule, and to arrange my stuff at perpendicular angles…and damn proud of it!

PERFECTIONISM IS FLAWED.

THE THIRD ACT

"Welcome to sixty…for it is the springtime of your old age." Such was the birthday greeting I received from my friend, Louie (who, not incidentally, was several years older than I when he sent it).

Getting older is an endless series of accommodations — to one's expectations, hopes, dreams, and most acutely, health. Things we cavalierly took for granted in our youth insidiously become the stuff of ancient history.

Gone are the days when, no matter what the ailment, you'd go to see your doctor, and, nine times out of ten, you were sent away with a bemused, "You're *fine*, now *get outta here!*" Over the ensuing decades, that ratio gradually reverses, to where it eventually becomes the exception, rather than the rule. You come to expect previously unheard-of phrases such as, "I'm not sure," or "Let's keep an eye on this," or, perhaps most disheartening of all, "Yeah, that happens."

Early one spring morning, I made my routine post-coffee sojourn to the bathroom and — um, let's see, how shall I put this? — I noticed a distinctly different "hue" than the one to which I had grown accustomed over the previous six decades of my life. I wouldn't say that I was exactly alarmed…but, frankly, I was exactly alarmed. In a state of quasi-controlled panic, I immediately rushed in to see my doctor. He calmly informed me that there are lots of possible causes, and he patiently waded through his Q&A checklist. It started out innocently enough. "Eating beets or rhubarb?" "No." "Dehydrated from exercise?" "No." "In any discomfort or pain?" "No." And so it went, back and forth. Finally, he emitted the sound that I have come to dread from doctors: "Hmm." I tried to appear composed, belying the visible thumping in my chest. "So Doc, what do you think?" I vaguely remember him saying something about running some labs and getting a CAT scan, and that it might be kidney stones…but it could be *something else*. "Like what?" I choked out, desperately trying to convince myself that he wasn't going to say what I knew he was going to say anyway. "Well," he began, "we want to make sure it isn't cancer." I swallowed… hard. He tried to reassure me by telling me that even though I wasn't in any pain, it still could be kidney stones. But the only thing that resonated in my head was "cancer." ("*Cancer*"!?)

Now, I'd suffered the unadulterated agony of kidney stones before. I am convinced that Satan himself took particular delight as he cunningly designed these evil little burrs of torture — which ever-so-sadistically and ever-so-slowly carve and slice their way down the delicate tissues of your tiny, unsuspecting ureter tubes, burrowing toward their inevitable destination to you-know-where. You are unceremoniously stripped of all pride and dignity, driven from your feet, then to your knees, then to the floor, reduced to a pathetic mass of sniveling, writhing protoplasm. It's an excruciating ordeal that I wouldn't wish on my worst enemy. (Okay, well maybe my *worst* enemy…)

So, it was down to this: kidney stones or cancer. Mind you the CAT scan was no stroll on the beach — the cold intravenous dye, the physical immobility, the claustrophobia. But none of that compared to the agony of waiting…and waiting…and waiting for the results.

When my doctor finally contacted me with the outcome, I was flooded with emotion, and instinctively called my mother. "Mom, I have *great* news, I've got kidney stones!" (And I *meant* it.) "Thank God! David, I am so happy for you!" (And *she* meant it.)

As you get older, you keep lowering your standards for what is acceptable. And in the third act, the absence of catastrophic news is great news.

LIFE LESSON:

WITH AGE,
THE ABSENCE OF
CATASTROPHIC
NEWS IS GREAT NEWS.

FINAL REQUEST

It was a bad diagnosis. A very bad diagnosis. *Pancreatic cancer.* We all knew what that meant. Especially for my eighty-two-year-old dad. "The lowest survival rate of all twenty-one common cancers," the oncologist informed us, trying unsuccessfully to strike a balance between objective professional and caring human. "Surgery is your only real chance to save him. But given his age and condition, it's a big risk. We can't be sure that he'll even survive the operation."

The thought of losing my dad gripped my throat like a vice, barely allowing any air to squeeze into my lungs. I could only imagine how my mom was feeling. They had been together since they were teenagers. And it had all come down to this. But it didn't feel like we really had much choice; no one could bear the thought of watching him painfully waste away. So, the surgery was on. He signed page after page of paperwork, including his directive that, should things go wrong, there were to be no extraordinary medical measures taken to keep him alive. In other words: "Just let me die."

Weeks passed, and the fateful day finally arrived. We — my mom, my brother, my sister, and I — spent that morning in his hospital room huddled around his bed, trying our best to smile and act cheerful. But the air was thick with fear and sadness.

The minutes both crawled and flew by. A rabbi came into the room to offer a pre-surgery blessing. My dad — a longtime avowed atheist — even seemed moved by the undeniable feeling of something spiritual that seemed to permeate the room. Finally, it was time. They showed up with the gurney to wheel him off. We were seeing him for maybe the last time. Ever. My dad looked up at my sister and asked, "Do you still have that document, sweetheart? About not taking any measures to keep me alive?" "Yes, I do Dad," said my sister, choking back tears. "Good," he responded. "*Tear it up.*" Yes, we laughed. Yes, we cried. And yes, he survived the surgery. Modern medicine is truly a miracle — but no more than the remarkable will to live. And my dad simply was not ready to go…

LIFE LESSON:

NEVER UNDERESTIMATE THE WILL TO LIVE.

EPILOGUE

THE SHOT — REDUX

"It is what it is." For decades, I'd bristle at the very utterance of that blazingly obvious, circular, overused phrase. I mean, how could "it" be other than what it is? How could it be what it *isn't*? The whole thing just seemed to be nothing more than a worthless, pseudo-metaphysical pretzel.

That is, until I glimpsed a post-game interview with an NBA star in the twilight of his career. Love him or hate him, indifferent to him or (somehow) unaware of him, Kobe Bryant was a superhuman force to behold throughout the span of his remarkable athletic reign. His talent. His skills. His will to win. And, not incidentally, his ability to play through utterly incapacitating pain. The litany of injuries he endured is mind boggling: multiple fractured fingers and knees, torn shoulder, ruptured Achilles tendon, and a never-ending array of maladies to his back, hip, and ankles. And through it all, Kobe just kept ferociously competing — and usually winning. After a particularly grueling game, the interviewer queried him, "How are you consistently able to perform, despite all your body has been through?" Kobe took only a brief moment to ponder the question. With a shrug of his shoulders and a tilt of his head, he replied, "it's just pain."

It's just pain. He didn't offer up an elaborate or convoluted explanation. He wasn't trying to elicit pity or admiration. His use of the word "just" didn't minimize the extent of the pain (which, I'm certain, was excruciating). No, "just" meant "simply." As in, "it's nothing more than that." As in, "that's all it is." As in, "*it is what it is.*"

In that moment, I got it. The phrase "it is what it is" finally rang true for me as a useful mindset, not just a worthless cliché. It meant "don't make something more of it than it already is" — even if the "it" might be painful, confusing, scary, or otherwise troubling.

However, I came to realize that "it" can actually metamorphize into something much more...the moment we find personal meaning in it. When Nurse Gabe stabbed me with that shot at age six, it was really painful — and then it wasn't. In that sense, getting a shot simply was what it was. But, what did I take from that experience? It taught me that, when faced with the inevitable, it's best to just face it and get it over with.

When we derive some kind of meaning from our experiences, they can all become valuable life lessons. Like learning when a tie is really a win. Or striving for simplicity. Or recognizing the limits of insight. Or sometimes just stating the obvious. Or cherishing the journey more than the destination. Or surviving betrayal. Or admiring the will to live.

All of our experiences are what they are — plus the meaning we attach to or reap from them. And that includes the meaning we experience by sharing it with others — as I'm doing with you right now…

LIFE LESSON:

IT IS WHAT YOU MAKE OF IT.

APPENDIX

"THE LESSONS"

Author's Note: This is a list of the key life lessons I learned from each story. You might have taken different ones...

The Shot
When you have to face the inevitable,
it's best just to get it over with.

The Challenge
Sometimes a tie is really a win.

The Nature of Attachment
Doing the right thing can be painful.

The Empty Threat
Empty threats are worse than none at all.

Bridging the Racial Divide
Life isn't fair — but it's easier with companionship.

"...And Nothing but the Truth"
Defeat rationalizations with truth.

Worse and Worser
Things could always be worse.

The Zen Stripper
Living in the moment makes life manageable.

Testing the Limits
You only know you've gone too far when you've gone too far.

A Short Story
Try to replace envy with self-acceptance.

The Ticking Clock
You risk losing the present by fretting about the future.

The Stoned Wall
Recognize the limits of your own control.

The Marvels of Cynicism
A healthy dose of cynicism is a potent antidote against gullibility.

Kiss Quest
Simple is better — but not always easier.

Passing the Ultimate Buck
Some gaps can never be bridged.

The Impostor Syndrome
When you don't know what to do, fake it 'til you make it.

15-Zip
It's all a matter of scale.

Hedonic Greed
Beware the illusion of choice.

The Shell Game
If it seems too good to be true, it probably is.

Empathic Failure
Find forgiveness through empathy.

Tincture of Time
The two best healers are Mother Nature and Father Time.

It's Just a Four-Letter Word
The answers to some questions are destined to remain unknowable.

Uncool Effort
Try hard — but not too hard.

The Booby Prize
Insight has frustrating limits.

Obviously
There are merits to just sticking with the basics.

Inverted Self-Esteem
Have the wisdom not to fight every battle.

When Intuition Goes Awry
Learn when to trust facts over feelings.

The Prozac Dilemma
Every decision involves trade-offs.

Pseudo-Worries
It's easier to worry about things we can control than things we can't.

"He Just Doesn't Understand"
'Tis better to solve than to complain.

Lying or Crazy?
Differentness in itself is not a threat.

"We Hold These Truths…"
Love is a self-evident truth.

Biofeedback
Your body is the conduit to your emotions.

Journey B. Goode
The journey can be more satisfying than the destination.

To Love, Honor, and Betray
The experience of betrayal accentuates the value of loyalty.

Zorro Goes Home
Love something enough to let it go.

Perfectly Flawed
Perfectionism is flawed.

The Third Act
With age, the absence of catastrophic news is great news.

Final Request

Never underestimate the will to live.

The Shot — Redux

It is what you make of it.

(P. S. If these lessons seem too obvious, please take a look at the story titled "Obviously"!)

P.S.

I sincerely hope that you enjoyed this book. In my experience, writers want (sometimes desperately!) to connect with their readers — and I am no exception. I would like for this experience to be as interactive as possible. Along these lines, you have a standing invite to post your own life lesson stories on my Facebook group page, LIFE IS A 4-LETTER WORD. For your interest, as a special "bonus feature," I've also included a bunch of real-life photos from these stories on my website davidlevypsych.com, under Scrapbook.

I welcome all reader feedback. If you like the book, please let me know (david@davidlevypsych.com) and post a review on Amazon. If you didn't like it, then, well, don't forget what your mother once told you about, "If you can't say something nice…"

Thanks for reading!

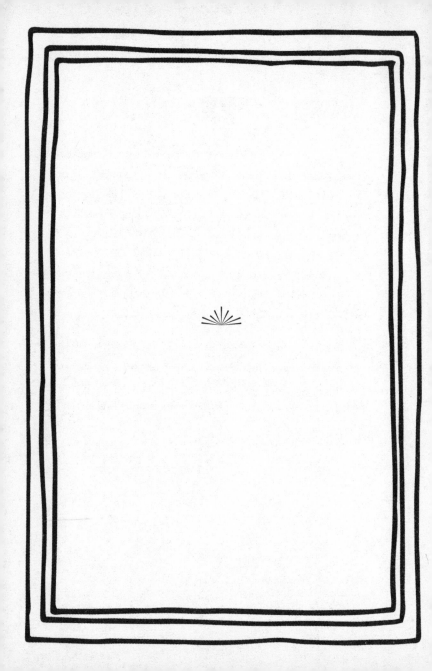

ACKNOWLEDGMENTS

This book was over sixty-five years in the making. It reflects the culmination of a lifetime of personal experiences, reflections, and learning. I am indebted to the countless individuals who have — wittingly or unwittingly — shaped my journey and, as a consequence, these stories. This book could never have been realized without their contributions.

Although many authors have significantly influenced my thinking and writing, those I still find to be especially valuable include Viktor Frankl, Thomas Szasz, R. D. Laing, George Orwell, Joseph Heller, Ambrose Bierce, Frank O'Connor, Eudora Welty, Hans Eysenck, Paul Meehl, William Goldman, Neil Simon, Jules Feiffer, and, of course, Margaret Wise Brown and Dr. Seuss. Inspiration of a different kind was provided by the insights, humor, and wisdom of Gary Larson, Matt Groening, B. Kliban, Leigh Rubin, and, when I was a miserable teenager, MAD Magazine.

It's one thing to collect a bunch of anecdotes and occasionally disclose them to friends, students, or even clients. However, it's quite another to transform them into a book that I hope to share with a wide range of readers. That's where the following individuals come in...

Thank you to my agent, Beth Davey, and my manager, John Tomko, for enthusiastically believing in this project from the outset, and to Hayes Jackson for forging the initial connection. My deep gratitude extends to every member of my "A+ Team": Susie Stangland (social media guru), Emi Battaglia (publicist), and Lucinda Dyer and Bryan Azorsky at Nodebud Authors (website designers). A special shout out goes to my invaluable (and remarkably tolerant) research assistants Dianne Kong, Alexander Lewin, Dawne Czarny, and Sandy Sayah-Pedram.

It is with great pleasure that I take this opportunity to acknowledge the creative input and tremendous support I received at virtually every stage of this book's development from the superb professionals at Mango Publishing, particularly Brenda Knight (associate publisher), Chris McKenney (CEO), Robin Miller (editor), Elina Diaz (graphic designer), Scott McKenney (book titler extraordinaire), Hannah Jorstad Paulsen (marketing manager), and Merritt Smail (sales and marketing assistant).

Thanks to those friends, family, and associates who offered their insights and feedback on various versions of my manuscript: Lynne Wetzell, Annie Wharton, Drew Erhardt, Andrea Levy, Marilee Bradford, Jonathan "JP" Perpich, Barbara Ingram, Steve Nevil, Robert Levy, Sherrie Basch Stelik, Arielle Eckstut, and Laura Munson. I also wish to acknowledge the love and support of my "step-kids," Katherine Sauska, Jaclyn Tebbe, Kerry Tebbe, and Christian Sauska; my "step-grandkids," Christian, August, and Giorgia Sauska; and the pets I've cherished throughout my life, Samantha, Lucy, Emma, and Zorro.

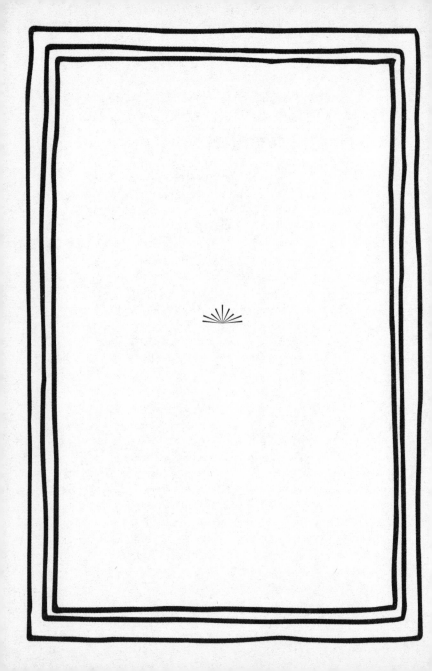

ABOUT THE AUTHOR

Dr. David A. Levy has extensive experience as a professor, therapist, author, actor, researcher, and media consultant.

Professor and Therapist

Levy is a Professor of Psychology at Pepperdine University, where he has been teaching graduate psychology courses since 1986. He received his BA degree in theater arts from UCLA, his MA in psychology from Pepperdine University, a second MA in psychology from UCLA, and his PhD in psychology from UCLA, where he specialized in social psychology. He served as a Visiting Professor of Psychology in the Soviet Union, where he delivered lectures and workshops at Leningrad (now St. Petersburg) State University and the Leningrad Academy of Science. He was honored as a Harriet and Charles Luckman

Distinguished Teaching Fellow and with the Howard A. White Award for Teaching Excellence at Pepperdine and was a recipient of the Shepard Ivory Franz Distinguished Teaching Award and Charles F. Scott Fellowship at UCLA. Dr. Levy holds professional licenses both in psychology and in marriage and family therapy and has worked in a wide range of private practice and inpatient settings.

Author and Researcher

Levy's book, *Tools of Critical Thinking*, (acclaimed as "the thinking person's self-help book"), garnered widespread acclaim for its innovative approaches to improving thinking skills. Levy coauthored (with Eric Shiraev) *Cross-Cultural Psychology: Critical Thinking and Contemporary Applications* (currently in its 6th edition), which has become an international bestselling textbook and has been translated into four foreign languages. Levy is the author of *Family Therapy: History, Theory, and Practice*, which was the first textbook on the topic available to Russian readers. His numerous theoretical and empirical research studies have been published in scientific journals and presented at professional conferences.

Satirist

Levy has published numerous satirical articles, including "How to Be a Good Psychotherapy Patient," "The Emperor's Postmodern Clothes," "Psychometric Infallibility Realized: The

One-Size-Fits-All Psychological Profile," "Stinks and Instincts: An Empirical Investigation of Freud's Excreta Theory," and "A Proposed Category for the Diagnostic and Statistical Manual of Mental Disorders (DSM): Pervasive Labeling Disorder."

Media Experience

As a media consultant, Levy has appeared on over seventy television and radio broadcasts (including CNN, CBS, NBC, PBS, NPR, Fox, NatGeo, A&E, and E!), providing psychological perspectives on current events, and examining issues and trends in the mental health fields.

He has also worked as a professional director, producer, writer, and actor in motion pictures, television, and stage. He received an Emmy nomination for Outstanding Performance in a Network Television Series, and he was a guest star on the television series "Cheers," where he portrayed the leader of Frasier's low self-esteem group (a role which he adamantly maintains is *not* "type-casting").